RAILS UNDER THE MIGHTY HUDSON

HUDSON VALLEY HERITAGE SERIES
Robert F. Jones, series editor

1. *Palisades: 100,000 Acres in 100 Years* by Robert O. Binnewies

RAILS
UNDER THE
MIGHTY HUDSON

The Story of the Hudson Tubes,
the Pennsy Tunnels
and Manhattan Transfer

by BRIAN J. CUDAHY

Fordham University Press
New York
2002

Copyright © 2002 by Brian J. Cudahy
All rights reserved
ISBN 0-8232-2189-X hardcover
ISBN 0-8232-2190-3 Paperback
ISSN 1534-1399

Hudson Valley Heritage Series, no. 2

Library of Congress Cataloging-in-Publication Data

Cudahy, Brian J.
    Rails under the mighty Hudson : the story of the Hudson Tubes, the Pennsy tunnels, and Manhattan Transfer / by Brian J. Cudahy.— 2nd ed.
       p.   cm. — (Hudson Valley heritage series ; 2)
    Includes bibliographical references and index.
    ISBN 0-8232-2189-X (hardcover) — ISBN 0-8232-2190-3 (pbk.)
    1. Railroad tunnels—New York (State)—History. 2. Railroad tunnels—New Jersey—History. I. Title. II. Series.
    TF230 .C8 2002
    385.3'12—dc21
                                                                                                              2001055605

Permission to quote from *Manhattan Transfer* by John Dos Passos, Houghton Mifflin Co., © 1925 and 1953, has been kindly granted by Mrs. John Dos Passos, the copyright holder.
    Special appreciation and thanks are tendered herewith to Harry Cotterell, Jr., of Newark, New Jersey, for his many comments and suggestions, and to B. J. Cunningham of North Miami, Florida, for permission to use the illustration from a Hudson & Manhattan Railroad stock certificate.

Printed in the United States of America

CONTENTS

Preface to the Second Edition	7
Prologue	9
Part One: The Hudson Tubes	10
Part Two: The New York Tunnel Extension	27
Part Three: Transition	55
Part Four: Into a New Century	81
Bibliography	97
Appendix A: Rapid Transit Roster	101
Appendix B: Electric Locomotives	102
Appendix C: Railroad Electric Multiple-Unit Cars	104
Appendix D: Departures from Penn Station	106

PREFACE TO THE SECOND EDITION

Rails Under the Mighty Hudson was first published in 1975 by Stephen Greene Press, of Brattleboro, Vermont. Those who enjoy anomalies might find it amusing to learn that a book whose subject matter was, at least in part, the Pennsylvania Railroad was published as part of a Stephen Greene series that dealt with U.S. short-line railroads.

Over the ensuing quarter-century, I have received steady correspondence about what was, all in all, a rather small book. But its dual subject matter—the Hudson Tubes, now known as the PATH System, and the Hudson River tunnels built by the Pennsy and today utilized by Amtrak and New Jersey Transit—are intriguing topics with perennial interest. Many asked if the book would ever be republished. Now it has been, and I am grateful to Fordham University Press for giving it a new home among its various Hudson Valley specialty titles.

About the new edition, I hasten to say the following. The revised edition incorporates as much of the original as was practical. An effort has been made to correct what I will euphemistically refer to as an imprecision or two in the earlier edition, and wording has been altered so the new edition does not speak in a 1975 voice. Part Four is an entirely new section that brings the narrative up to the turn of a new century. The selection of photographs has been updated and some new ones have been added. Appendix material has been revised; a bibliography and an index are now included.

As this revised edition of *Rails Under the Mighty Hudson* was being prepared for publication, the terrible events of September 11, 2001, came to pass. Because PATH rapid transit trains terminate directly below the World Trade Center, this important transport link under the Hudson River between lower Manhattan and New Jersey was rendered inoperable. At this writing in late October of 2001, its future is uncertain.

As with so many other New York institutions, PATH performed heroically on September 11. A PATH train from Newark arrived at the WTC Terminal minutes after the first jetliner struck One World Trade Center at 8:45 a.m. Passengers were told to remain on the train as doors were opened so people on the platform could get aboard; the train then quickly departed for the safety of New Jersey. A following train, with a full load of passengers, was ordered to proceed through the WTC Terminal without stopping and return directly to New Jersey. Then, with the horrific events still unfolding, PATH sent a train that was empty save for its engineer and conductor under the Hudson and into the WTC Terminal to evacuate any remaining passengers, as well as PATH employees. That last train arrived at the World Trade Center at 9:10, loaded up, and departed at 9:12.

PATH's rapid response in returning two trains to New Jersey, and preventing additional trains from entering the WTC Terminal, saved thousands of lives that awful morning. September 11, 2001, proved to be a day when heroism was anything but in short supply in New York.

Burke, Virginia
October 2001

Concourse level of the World Trade Center, where a bank of escalators led passengers down to PATH's WTC Terminal.

PROLOGUE

THERE WAS an old-time silent movie in which mustachioed comedian Chester Conklin stole the show. He played the role of an Alaskan prospector who struck it rich. His beautiful daughter was wooed and won by a city slicker. This son-in-law kept describing New York City and its wonders to the old man. Chester grudgingly accepted one incredibility after another, from skyscrapers to subways. Everything, that is, except the Hudson Tubes. Naw, there ain't no train can run *under* a river. B'gosh, the water'd put out the fire in the en-jine and drown all the people. Naw, I ain't gonna believe no such thing. It's agin nature.

They finally take the old man to New York, where a ride on rails under the mighty Hudson demonstrates that indeed it can be done. In the final scene, however, the camera pans from the lovers' embrace to Chester at a table watching a Lionel train encircle a loop of track. Shaking his head. Pulling his mustache. Still not quite convinced.

In truth, it took a long time to convince anybody that trains could run under a river. In the years after the American Civil War, so the stories go, Wall Street financiers were forever being badgered by a character known only as "Crazy Luke." He would wait long hours outside fashionable downtown clubs and restaurants, trying to steal a few minutes' attention from bankers and industrialists to argue a cause he zealously tried to promote. For "Crazy Luke" was interested in building a tunnel under the Hudson River from New York to New Jersey, a magnificent mile-long tube through which railroad trains could run, ending forever the insularity that separated Manhattan Island from, literally, the mainland of the United States.

They put Luke away in an asylum.

Steel engraving reproduced from H&M stock certificate depicts tube train burrowing under PRR's Exchange Place train shed, destination Hudson Terminal on lower Manhattan. (Courtesy of the late B. G. Cunningham)

Part One: THE HUDSON TUBES

THE HUDSON is an old river. Geologists estimate it dates to the so-called Cretaceous Period some 75 million years ago; during the later Tertiary Period it is thought that the river may have meandered somewhat from its present course in the area called Tappan Zee and actually reached the ocean on a course to the west of where the Jersey Palisades now stand. European eyes first gazed on the mighty Hudson in the sixteenth century, and the Hudson, both river and valley, has played a singular role in the unfolding tableau of American history.

Yet for all the aesthetic and economic advantages the Hudson has provided, crossing the river—from Manhattan to New Jersey—has always been a problem and a bother. Regular ferry lines date to Colonial times. Not the first, but possibly the best known of the various routes was the Hoboken Ferry, established in 1775, by a gentleman named Cornelius Rapelye.* The nineteenth century saw the deployment of steam-powered side-wheelers on the var-

---

* An arresting and entertaining little volume—although not easy to locate—is Harry J. Smith's *Romance of the Hoboken Ferry*, published by Prentice-Hall in 1931.

ious services; and as railroads were built inland from the Hudson, their schedules were dovetailed with the ferry lines. Without going into precisions of corporate law and interstate commerce, "mergers" of sorts were effected between the railroad companies and the older ferry lines. The Hoboken Ferry, for example, eventually became a marine subsidiary of the Delaware, Lackawanna and Western R R. It was this company's ferryboat *Bergen* which introduced a popular new technology to the Hudson ferry fleet just before the turn of the century. When the vessel was launched at Delamater Iron Works in Newburg, N.Y., in October of 1888, she was the first double-ended ferry to eschew side-wheel propulsion and employ a screw propeller successfully. "A more efficient means for crossing the river can scarcely be imagined," opined a contemporary account.

THE FIRST TUNNEL EFFORT

"Crazy Luke" was not the earliest man to dream of a subaqueous tunnel. Leonardo da Vinci's notebooks contain preliminary sketches of the equipment necessary to construct such a thing, and tunnel-building itself is an ancient and honorable art that goes back to the Babylonians and the earliest days of recorded history.

Recorded history also reveals that it was in 1874 that a transplanted Californian and former colonel in the Union Army named DeWitt Clinton Haskin actually began the first real effort to tunnel beneath the waters of the mighty Hudson. Haskin had traveled east through Omaha and was fascinated by a compressed-air-and-caisson system used to build piers for a Missouri River Bridge there. The technique involved a large inverted "box"—or caisson—which was positioned at the site of the pier. The masonry pier itself was constructed atop the caisson, which began to sink into the river bottom. Compressed air was fed into the chamber to keep watery slime beneath the open bottom of the caisson out of the interior. Here workmen toiled, under pressure, excavating the downward journey of the caisson, a journey which continued until bedrock, or some other solid material, was reached.

Why not an even larger-scale project using the same technique, thought Haskin? Why not an underwater tunnel?

In New York he sought out $10 million in financing from one Trevor Park and founded the Hudson Tunnel Railroad Company in 1873. In November of the following year a shaft was sunk for the proposed tunnel back from the bulkhead line of the Jersey Shore. But the project would go no further for five more years. On December 15, 1874 the Lackawanna Railroad secured an injunction against Haskin's company, and it was not until September of 1879 that actual digging commenced on the tunnel itself after litigation had run its course.

Plagued by financial and technical problems, the Haskin efforts were not to succeed. True, twelve hundred feet of brick-lined tunnel were eventually built out under the water from the Jersey Shore, and the technique of creating an artificially pressurized atmosphere at thirty-five pounds per square inch inside the a-building structure was employed, in imitation of the Missouri River project. What was not employed, though, was a large boring shield at the head end of the digging, a device that would later be demonstrated as the sine qua non for tunneling through soft silt. In other words, while the caisson technique worked well in building vertical bridge piers, when it came to digging a horizontal tunnel, problems developed. A "blowout" claimed twenty lives on July 21, 1880*. Some commentators were thankful when the pro-

---

* As with many tragedies, this one also produced heroism. When men in the airlock realized a "blowout" was imminent, they started for the pressurized door leading back to safety. Several were through when one Peter Woodland realized the loss of pressure in the tube was about to doom all, even those en route to

12

ject was eventually abandoned, since Haskin's original plan to run steam locomotives through the tunnel to a terminal near Washington Square would surely have induced massive asphyxiation in both train crews and passengers. Poor Haskin went to his grave a broken man, sightless and penniless.

In 1888, backed by British capital, a firm incorporated as the Hudson River Tunnel Company took up the task anew. It pushed the original tunnel forward another sixteen hundred feet or so, placing it very close to the Manhattan shore, and in addition began work on a parallel second tube. The contractor for this venture was S. Pearson and Sons, an English firm that had already won world-wide acclaim for the Forth Bridge in Scotland. In addition to money, Pearson brought a considerable amount of British know-how to the American side of the Atlantic. While bricks and mortar similar to those Haskin had used to construct the earlier tunnel were retained when work was re-activated on the trans-Hudson tube, the Pearson effort transformed tunnel building with an awesome import called the Greathead Shield. This circular device was named for its inventor, Sir James Henry Greathead, a South African-born British engineer who developed it initially for work on London's 1880 Tower Subway. The shield was later described as a "mechanical mole," and while Greathead did not actually invent the device, he did so notably perfect its performance that his name has ever since been associated with it. The Pearson firm set up Greathead Shields in the forward position of each tunnel, reducing the risk of pressure failure in the tubes and allowing work to proceed at a much faster—and safer—pace than Haskin ever dreamed possible. Withal, the Hudson River enterpise again failed, this time for financial reasons principally, and the project lay dormant for another span of years.

Enter Mr. McAdoo

In 1892, just about the time the British effort was coming to naught, a young Georgia-born lawyer out of Chattanooga, Tennessee, arrived in New York to seek fame and fortune. His name was William Gibbs McAdoo, a quiet man with extraordinary gifts who was described as tall and spare, with bushy eyebrows, deep-

safety. He closed the door, thereby sealing his own doom and that of the nineteen others in the airlock with him, but insuring safety for the men already on the way out. His action is memorialized on his tombstone in New York Bay Cemetery in Jersey City, and the incident itself later formed the basis for a famous short story by Theodore Dreiser entitled "St. Columba and the River."

William Gibbs McAdoo, posed on one of the electric "mules" used during tunnel construction. The mules were built by Baldwin Locomotive works, with electrical gear by Westinghouse. (Author's collection)

set eyes and a strong face. By way of similarities, many felt he had a decided Lincolnesque appearance. But it was not McAdoo's looks that were his dominant feature; it was energy, drive and ability to accomplish goals that have enshrined him in the halls of the mighty. Besides his legal training, McAdoo had a background in railroading; in later years, after serving first as President Wilson's Secretary of the Treasury, where he was instrumental in establishing the Federal Reserve System, he was named Director General of all American railroads when they were placed under government operation during World War I. Following this stint, McAdoo turned to elective politics on his own. He made vigorous tries for the Democratic nomination for president in 1920 and 1924; never daunted, in 1933, at the robust age of seventy, he was elected a United States Senator from the state of California, and he served until 1939.

In 1901 McAdoo's fancy was caught by the idea of a trans-Hudson tunnel even before he knew such a project had ever been attempted. One day while talking to John Dos Passos he casually mentioned what had been little more than a daydream, and Dos Passos, who lost money on one of the early attempts, outlined details of the aborted efforts. (This, by the way, was not novelist John *Roderigo* Dos Passos, but John *Randolph* Dos Passos, a noted lawyer who wrote extensively on the problem of trusts. Oddly enough, novelist Dos Passos will appear in a subsequent chapter of our narrative.) Quickly McAdoo contacted Frederick B. Jennings, the attorney for the bondholders. On a grey and depressing day in October of 1901, in the company of Charles M. Jacobs, an eminent engineer who had earlier constructed New York's very first subaqueous tunnel,* McAdoo descended the Haskin shaft in Jersey and made his way into the gloomy and abandoned tunnel excavation. Said McAdoo later: "The Fates had marked a day when I was to go under the riverbed and encounter this piece of dripping darkness, and it would rise from its grave and walk by my side. I was destined to give it color and movement and warmth, but it would change the course of my life and lead me into a new career."

McAdoo and Jacobs, dressed in hip boots and yellow oilskins, walked all the way to the rusting Greathead Shield, which Pearson had abandoned. Jacobs looked it over and declared it was mechanically in good order and could be put to use again.

McAdoo obtained financing for completing the Hudson tunnel project. While originally he spoke only of a single-tube crossing, in short order he expanded the scope of his project by a considerable measure. Instead of a mere railroad delivery tube, McAdoo envisioned a complex and massive rapid transit network using electric-powered cars that would link the many railroad terminals in Jersey with New York, thus rendering obsolete time-consuming ferryboat rides across the Hudson. In addition, McAdoo saw the line extending out across the Jersey Meadows and reaching the nearby city of Newark.

McAdoo, in other words, was enamored of the idea of building an electric interurban railway—but not in the sparsely settled flatlands of the Middle West, where such lines were becoming commonplace and would reach the zenith of their perfection. He was going to build his line around, through, and under the heavily populated New York metropolitan area and include in the right-of-way an underwater crossing of the Hudson River to boot. In fact, as plans began to develop after McAdoo paid $4 million to buy out the franchise of his ill-fated predecessor, his system would include not one, but *two*, twin-tube Hudson River tunnels. And maybe even more!

On Saturday, January 15, 1908, a group of invited guests left McAdoo's office at 111 Broadway and traveled uptown to Fourteenth Street on the Sixth Avenue El. The party descended a stair-

---

* An eight-foot wide tunnel under the East River built in 1894 to carry mains for the Ravenswood Gas Company.

way from the overhead rapid transit line and continued down another flight of stairs to a brand new underground station of something soon to be called the Hudson and Manhattan Railroad Company. There a train of eight all-steel, standard gauge, electric-powered, multiple-unit subway cars waited for them, and shortly after 4:00 P.M. the group embarked on a test ride under the Hudson River to Hoboken. The motorman for the trip was the H. & M.'s superintendent, one E. M. Hedley, a brother of the man who would later become president of the Interborough Rapid Transit Company, the firm founded by August Belmont which opened New York's very first subway in October of 1904.

Trains had begun hauling sandbags on test runs over a month earlier, and so the January 15 trip was not the first operation through the McAdoo Tunnels, as, to the infinite displeasure of the modest William G., the line came to be called. The fact remained, however, that McAdoo had conquered the Hudson River!

The original brick tunnel of the Haskin effort was retained and completed, for McAdoo's engineers were impressed with the quality of work that had been put into it. The parallel second tube which Pearson began could not be worked into a grade-separated underground junction near the Jersey shoreline, as planned, and it was sealed and abandoned.

The general level of safety on tunnel projects had improved

Construction scene in Morton Street tunnel as "sandhogs" advance the tube beneath the Hudson River. (Author's collection)

measurably since the days of D. C. Haskin. Prior to 1889, a full twenty-five percent of all workers who toiled inside a pressure lock died of the dreaded "bends." As medical knowledge advanced and the nature of the condition became known, preventive medicine was used to reduce this toll. Men in the primary airlock worked under a pressure of thirty-eight pounds per square inch. The bends—a condition of excessive nitrogen levels in the bloodstream—could be avoided if restoration of normal pressure (decompression) was at a sufficiently slow rate. One minute of decompression was recommended for each two pounds of pressure, for instance. Additionally, a "hospital lock" was constructed near the tunnel shaft; should a sandhog develop symptoms of the bends, he was placed inside, reintroduced to a pressurized atmosphere, and then decompressed at an even slower rate.

Construction was no easy task. Rock ledge was frequently encountered even in the deepest portions of the river bottom. At one time engineers were faced with the devastating prospect of a formation of reef rock that rose up twelve feet from the bottom of one of the tubes, a tube whose outside diameter was eighteen feet. In other words, while blasting was necessary at the bottom of the tunnel, the top had to be pushed forward through soft mud silt at the same time. A mere fifteen feet over the tunnel could be found, always, the waters of the Hudson River, totally unforgiving to those who did not pay scrupulous respect to the unnatural environment in which they were working. To help insure the safety of workers and the success of the project, barges of clay fill were dumped onto the river bottom atop the tunnel at spots where engineers were concerned about the danger of "blowouts."

Charles Jacobs was retained as chief engineer and he pioneered many novel construction techniques. Instead of allowing silt to ooze back through openings in the shield and then be carted out of the tunnel through the airlock aboard narrow-gauge rail cars, it was found the silt could be pushed to the sides of the shield, thereby decreasing costs and increasing the speed of construction. Another trick frequently used when the silt over the shield became too watery was to introduce hot torches into the tunnel and bake the silt into hard clay.

The general approach called for the use of two shields for each tube, aiming at a tricky mid-river rendezvous. Pearson had embarked on such a program years before, but since the original bore was very close to completion, McAdoo only activated work on one shield. On March 11, 1904—404 days after McAdoo's efforts had begun—the tunnel was "holed through," meeting up with a tunnel heading out from the New York shore left over from the Pearson project. A special telephone line had been installed to summon McAdoo at the magic moment, and when his boss arrived in the tunnel, Jacobs greeted him with: "Mr. McAdoo, we've something to show you." The two of them made their way through a door in the shield. Remarked McAdoo later, in words not dissimilar in spirit from those astronaut Neil Armstrong would use on a ceremonial occasion sixty-five years after: "For the first time in the history of mankind, men had walked on land from New Jersey to New York."

The next day, Saturday, March 12, an exuberant William McAdoo led a party of reporters on a trip through the bore. It had to be as strange and eerie a journey as working newsmen have ever made this side of a Jules Verne novel. From the foot of Cedar Street they were taken to the Jersey side aboard the tugboat *John Nichols*. Enroute, McAdoo pointed to an American flag flying at the foot of Morton Street and remarked: "That's where we'll come out." "If . . ." began a fearful reporter, but McAdoo cut in with a quip before he could articulate his misgivings.

A company surgeon gave the reporters a fast physical before allowing them inside the airlock; one burly man was rejected as unfit and not allowed to continue the tour, much to his own satisfaction. The rest then donned oilskins, boots and sou'westers, and for the next hour and a quarter made their way through the tube. First, it was down the Jersey shaft in an elevator, then a short ride out under the river aboard a narrow-gauge rail car. When they reached the airlock, McAdoo remarked that he and his company had frequently felt "pressure" from the press. "Now try some of ours," said he as the group entered the lock.

The entire enterprise McAdoo headed up was no small financial undertaking. In 1906, for instance, outstanding obligations were re-financed and certain previously separate corporations merged. The new bond issue was for $100 million, an extremely sizable tender for the day. Its rapid subscription is testimony to the enviable reputation McAdoo had by then established on Wall Street.

The second, or downtown tubes, linking Exchange Place, Jersey City, with Cortlandt Street in Manhattan, were begun in January of 1906. Placed in service in 1909, they terminated at a massive railway-owned office complex on Church Street, and the tenants that quickly signed up for space in the twin twenty-two-story

A train of H&M A-class cars in the Morton Street tunnel under the Hudson River prior to the institution of regular service in 1908. Iron segmental linings used to build the tunnels are evident. (Author's collection)

towers read like a litany of the nation's leading industrial firms. "The purchasing of this plot of ground," remarked McAdoo, "would have taxed the skill of a dozen diplomats, but somehow or other our brokers managed it."

Oddly, the Hudson Tubes were principally regarded as a Jersey enterprise. New Yorkers tended to treat the whole business with more than a slight bit of arrogance; after all, their Interborough subway was clearly the big leagues when it came to rapid transit, and the upstarts from across the river could be tolerated and even encouraged, but always in a patronizing way. Consider, for instance, this remark from *The New York Times* when a reporter was describing the many handgrips the new H&M cars featured: "They may become popular when the Hoboken and Jersey cut-ups go back home after a night in Manhattan."

Cars For the Tubes

When the H&M turned to the question of rolling stock to begin trans-Hudson service, three criteria were laid down. The cars had to be completely fireproof, they had to allow fast entry and exit, and they had to be as light in weight as possible. This was not an easy bill of particulars to fill, but a team headed by consultant L. B. Stillwell came up with a highly satisfactory design, and fifty cars were initially ordered—forty from A.C.F. and ten from Pressed Steel. They measured 48 feet in length, 8½ feet in width, and scaled in at 64,000 pounds, empty. Longitudinal seating was employed, and rather than combustible rattan, upholstery was woven out of a fireproof substance called "metal fabric." Floors were finished in cement, and carborundum particles were imbedded in the cement to render it less slippery. Externally the steel sides of the cars were built with thick vertical ribs to simulate the more luxurious wooden railroad cars of the day. Windows were arranged in pairs, and the upper sash curved into a gentle arch. Three large sliding doors were cut into each side—one at each of the end vestibules and one in the center of the car.

Once the full H&M system was complete, and multiple terminals in operation, correct identification of approaching trains would become quite important. Set into the ends of the roof monitor of H&M cars were a pair of identification lamps. Each was equipped with four colored discs—red, white, green and orange. Color codes were worked out so passengers could tell at a glance where a given train was going. Double red was always the set for the tail end of a train, and four oil lamps were hung at floor level—two white on the head end and two red on the rear.

The original cars were equipped with MCB-type trucks built by Baldwin Locomotive Works, one a "power" truck featuring two 100 hp GE #76 motors, and the other an "idler" truck. Current was drawn from an over-riding third rail, and Van Dorn couplers were used.

Many H&M rolling stock features were decided improvements on the four-year-old Interborough fleet, and even the shy Mr. McAdoo was known to brag about his system now and again, dwelling with special delight on all the innovations that August Belmont had yet to adopt for his Manhattan–Bronx subway, but that were standard equipment in the Hudson Tubes.

OPENING DAY

At 3:40:30 P.M. on Tuesday, February 25, 1908, the new line marked its formal and official opening. A nine-car train, one more than platform length could accommodate, was positioned in the station at Sixth Avenue and West Nineteenth Street (the line was still under construction beyond this point to its eventual terminal at Thirty-third Street) and a few minutes before the initiation, a telegraph message was tapped out from the platform to the incumbent of the White House, Theodore Roosevelt.

"The first official train of the Hudson and Manhattan Railway Company under the Hudson River awaits your signal and your pleasure. W. G. McAdoo."

While the message was being sent, power was shut off in the third rail at Nineteenth Street. Many aboard were impressed that the train did not then fall into total darkness; the cars were equipped with a 60-volt battery-powered emergency lighting system, still another feature the older Interborough then lacked.

At his desk in the White House, "TR" received McAdoo's message and pushed a button; this transmitted a signal to the railway's Manhattan substation, and power was restored to the third rail at the nominal direction of the nation's Chief Executive.

Then the inaugural special was off for Hoboken, with Chief Motorman Winkley at the controls. McAdoo remarked that "in the cool, under-river air there was a faint smell of varnish, of cement, of freshness, of things newly finished." Aboard was an impressive collection of dignitaries, most of whom kept their gold pocket watches out for the entire trip, timing the special's progress. Their Excellencies, Governors Charles Evans Hughes and Franklin Fort, of New York and New Jersey respectively, stood transfixed at the front window of the train for the entire 10½-minute ride, a ride that took them through the H&M's westbound tunnel, the very bore that was begun some thirty-odd years before by D. C.

Head-end lights gleaming in the rain, two H&M "black cars" drift into Journal Square, their trip from Thirty-third Street nearly complete. (Photo by author)

Haskin. Although the H&M had tacked on the ninth car in an effort to accommodate all invited guests, many notables had to stand, including Edward H. Harriman and Cornelius Vanderbilt III. The Commodore's grandson was twitted by his friends over this unlikely situation, but he responded with aplomb: "I would rather ride under the Hudson today hanging to a strap than ride to Albany in a private car."

At the state line, ninety-odd feet beneath mean high water, an illuminated arch of red, white and blue bulbs marked the midpoint of the 5650-foot tunnel, and when the train arrived in Hoboken, a crowd estimated at over ten thousand was on hand at street level to hear the oratory and celebrate the big event. McAdoo read a message from President Roosevelt, who had been invited to attend but did not: "The tunneling of the Hudson River is indeed a notable achievement," wrote the former Rough Rider, "one of those achievements of which all Americans are, as they should be, justly

H&M A-class cars in the railroad's Hoboken Terminal shortly after the line opened in 1908. (Author's collection)

proud." In a world of increasing instability, it is reassuring to note that the style of Presidential rhetoric seems to be a highly immutable commodity.

Walter K. Oakman, president of the Hudson Companies, a McAdoo subsidiary which handled construction of the tube, passed title to the Hudson and Manhattan Railroad Company, and John Bigelow, a former minister to the Court of Saint James and, at ninety-one, the oldest person to ride the H&M's first train, remarked to reporters that had he, as a youth, ever suggested that one day he might cross the Hudson beneath the riverbed, he would surely have been "pronounced a lunatic." Bigelow's daughter, Grace, was the only female aboard the inaugural train.

That night a formal dinner was held at Sherry's in New York for the VIP's but out in the snowy cold of Hoboken, with fireworks lighting the night sky, crowds began to queue up awaiting the opening of the tubes to the general public, scheduled for the uncivilized hour of midnight. Mrs. Barbara Schlatter of Hoboken was rewarded for her patience and became the very first patron to purchase a ticket on the new line. When the first New York-to-Hoboken train arrived at the Jersey terminal at 12:14, two men—Richard Scully and John Gladner—came sprinting up the stairs, competing vigorously for the honor of being the first person to complete fully a westbound transit under the Hudson on a scheduled train. Gladner won.*

Speaking of records, the H&M will, in its history, achieve a disproportionate number of rapid transit "firsts." But one significant mark it did not capture was that of being the first line to institute regular passenger service through a major underwater tunnel in New York. Belmont's Interborough began running under the East River—Bowling Green to Brooklyn—a month earlier.

EARLY DAYS ON THE H&M

There were many features of the Hudson Tubes that deserve mention. Under Sixth Avenue in Manhattan, for instance, the two tunnels were completely separated from each other; engineers pointed out this would afford much better ventilation of the tube,

---

* "Sprinting up the stairs" at Hoboken would become a time-honored ritual for passengers. Grab a newspaper after leaving the office and board the train in Manhattan; nervous glaces at one's watch as the H&M motorman makes his way for Hoboken. "Will I catch the 5:17?" Finally, the terminal—with less than a minute to go. At one time there was even an exit surcharge of a few pennies to delay matters still more. Then a mad dash up the stairs, into the DL&W concourse, and onto a train for South Orange or Montclair.

since approaching trains would act "like a piston" in circulating fresh air through tunnels and stations. It should be noted that adequate ventilation of underground tunnels was one of the most bothersome problems at the turn of the century for all new subway lines. Such concern is very understandable, for pulmonary disease was man's most deadly and feared killer at the time.

Underwater trackage was all protected by automatic train-stop signals. In later years, this safety feature would be extended to the entire system. Original plans called for the uptown crossing to feed into not one but two Manhattan delivery subways. These were to be the constructed line up Sixth Avenue, plus another, which was never completed, that would have branched off near Ninth Street and terminated on the east side of Manhattan in the vicinity of Fourth Avenue and Astor Place. To this day a tunnel heading can be seen east of the Ninth Street Station that was to have carried the proposed line.

When the full system was completed, two underground "flying junctions" inland from the Jersey shoreline drew much comment in the trade press, and magazines such as *Scientific American* never failed to celebrate all the line's engineering marvels. Another innovation the H&M pioneered was separate loading and unloading platforms at major terminals, a luxury the Interborough sorely missed. And discussion of stations is incomplete without mention of the Exchange Place facility, a huge underground cavern hacked out of solid rock some eighty-five feet below ground. Anglophiles may note the fact it is the closest thing in North America to a typical tube station on the London Underground.

McAdoo had several important triumphs to his credit during the H&M's early years. One key deal was the consummation of a partnership with the mighty Pennsylvania Railroad in 1903 whereby the Tubes would connect first with the railroad's Exchange Place terminal on the west bank of the Hudson and later with its main line out in the Jersey Meadows, and provide transfer service to downtown Manhattan for Pennsy's passengers.* Another was the gaining of a franchise, in 1909, to extend the H&M's

---

* In McAdoo's autobiography, *The Crowded Years*, he describes how he traveled to Philadelphia in early 1903 to meet Pennsylvania R R President Alexander J. Cassatt. After an hour with the persuasive McAdoo, the man who headed one of the most powerful corporations in the world agreed to transfer arrangements with an upstart electric railway that would not run its first train for five more years. "We'll hook up with you," Cassatt said. A formal agreement was signed three years later.

Interior view of a typical H&M rapid transit car, circa 1910.

route from its original Thirty-third Street terminal up Sixth Avenue to Bryant Park and then across to Grand Central Terminal on Forty-second Street. This action served to fuel rumors that McAdoo was on the verge of winning operational rights for at least some, if not all, of the new subway lines the City of New York was ready to build. Yet a third coup was nipping in the bud an attempt on the part of the Public Service Corporation of New Jersey to build a parallel and competitive Newark–New York high-speed transit line.

But perhaps the most significant feature of the H&M during its early years was the plaudits it earned for the calibre of service offered the public. McAdoo was adamant in demanding courteous deportment from his carefully selected corps of employees, and in direct opposition to the notorious adage ascribed to William H. Vanderbilt—"The Public Be Damned"—McAdoo adopted the slogan "The Public Be Pleased." Foreign-language timetables were distributed aboard New York-bound ocean liners while they were still at sea, and aggressive advertising campaigns were undertaken to insure maximum ridership on the tubes.

H&M dispatched trains from Nineteenth Street until the line was finished north to Thirty-third. Uniformed guards man their "chopper boxes" in this scene taken less than two weeks after service began. (PATH)

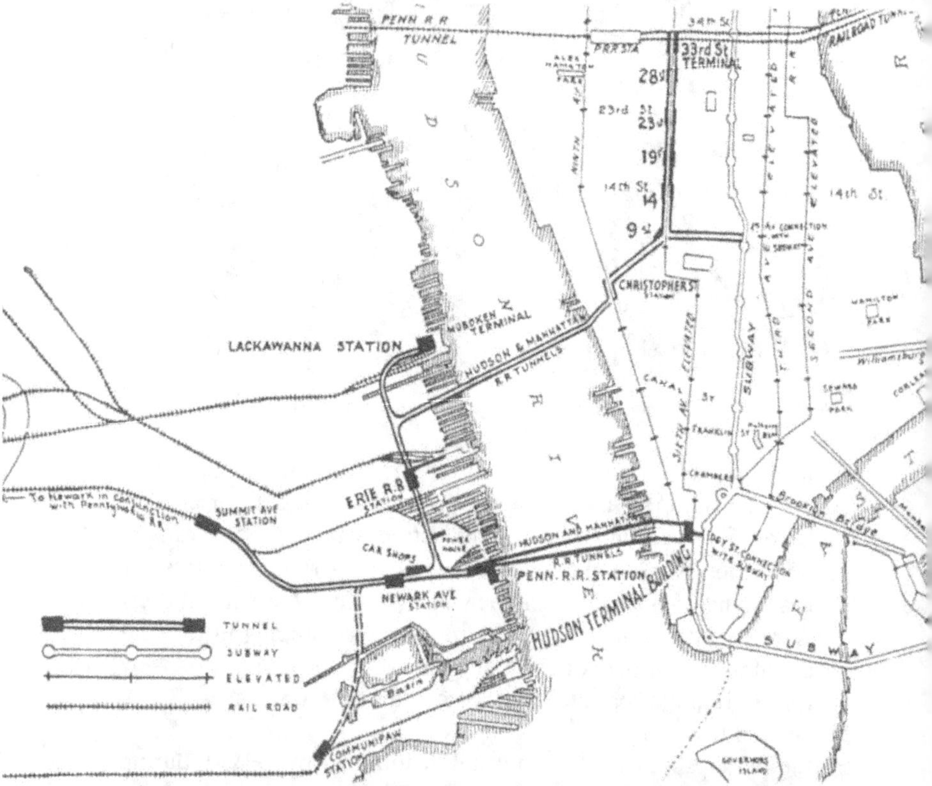

Top: Map of the Hudson and Manhattan, including never-built extensions to Communipaw, in Jersey City, and Fourth Avenue, in Manhattan. Bottom: Entrance gates in New York's Hudson Terminal announce service to both local points along the H&M as well as long-distance PRR connections at Manhattan Transfer.

Part Two: THE NEW YORK TUNNEL EXTENSION

MCADOO'S H&M was not the only railway company to burrow beneath the Hudson River in the early years of the twentieth century. The Pennsylvania Railroad was another—the only other.

The conflict out of which this part of our story develops began even before the Civil War, and involved all the principal Eastern railroads. The overall situation was that each railroad company had established a kind of territorial franchise at a particular East Coast seaport and was anxious to maintain its position. The B&O reigned supreme in Baltimore, the Pennsylvania called Philadelphia home, and Commodore Vanderbilt's New York Central and Hudson River Railroad was firmly entrenched to the north in a place that used to be called New Amsterdam. The villian of the piece was the always vexing question of freight rate differentials. Since Philadelphia, and more so Baltimore, faced higher ocean costs on the longer sea route to Europe, the "home" railroads were anxious to compensate for their disadvantage by keeping rail rates from the midwest to these cities lower than corresponding tariffs to New York. The Pennsylvaina Railroad at one time even made a move into the shipping business directly by founding its own steamship line in order to insure continued viability for the port of Philadelphia.* But New York had the greater clout, and it soon became apparent that import-export traffic was being monopolized by Gotham. Home-town loyalty gave way to business savvy, and in 1871 the Pennsylvania Railroad extended service across the flatlands of New Jersey to the banks of the Hudson and the doorstep of New York City.

It was freight traffic principally that motivated the Pennsylvania's migration to the northeast. But once lines were in place, passenger service quickly became the more glamorous commodity.

---

* The firm was called the American Line, a corporate forerunner of today's United States Line.

A large terminal complete with vaulted trainshed in the classic mold was built in the Paulus Hook section of Jersey City opposite Cortlandt Street, Manhattan, and over the years the service evolved into a principal means of travel between New York and the west and south.

Still there was the river. While the rival New York Central was able to bring New York-bound passengers directly onto Manhattan Island via the Hudson Valley route from the north and west, the mighty Pennsylvania was forced to transfer passengers to a fleet of double-ended ferryboats at Exchange Place (Paulus Hook) for the final mile or so of their ride. This may have been tolerable and even adequate for an Erie or a Jersey Central or a Lackawanna. But the Pennsylvania felt it was made of more noble stuff and refused to rest content until it, too, could establish a beachhead for its passengers on Manhattan Island.

Freight traffic, on the other hand, was afforded no competitive disadvantage by the Jersey quarantine since goods, and even entire railroad cars, could be placed aboard barges and lightered to waiting steamships anyplace in the harbor. But for its passengers Pennsy sought a better alternative.

For over three decades the railroad explored ways and means of crossing the Hudson. During these same years the company grew and prospered and became one of the nation's leading industrial firms, and quite possibly the most powerful and important railroad in the land.

As the nineteenth century entered its final decade, tunnel-building was still a risky and venturesome business. While there were earlier developments in Europe, the first subaqueous bore to carry traffic in North America was beneath the St. Claire River, through which trains of the Grand Trunk RR started on the international run from Sarnia, Ontario, to Port Huron, Michigan, in 1890. The second "travel tunnel" did not open until 1904 when trolley cars of the Boston Elevated Railway began to make their way from Maverick Square in East Boston, under the harbor to Court Street station in Boston proper. The Pennsylvania was more than passingly interested in the efforts of our old friend DeWitt Clinton Haskin, but the railroad was not about to lend its prestige to so untested an idea.

In the 1880's talk turned to a Hudson River bridge—inspired, likely, by the successful opening of Brooklyn Bridge in '83—with plans for such a project actually developed by Gustav Lindenthal. The War Department, however, quashed it: a threat to navigation.

After some maneuvering, Congress passed legislation which might well have removed the earlier objections, but the project had ballooned to unmanageable proportions—at one point, *fourteen* railroad tracks were proposed—and would have required the cooperation of nearly all the railroads terminating on the west bank of the Hudson. They were either unable or unwilling to participate, PRR felt it could not go such a project alone, and so the Hudson remained inviolate.

With the advent of the twentieth century, tunnel-building started to become a slightly less risky undertaking. Having examined a proposal to build a line off the Pennsylvania main in Jersey, over a bridge to Staten Island, under the Narrows to Brooklyn, and then into Manhattan via an East River tunnel, Pennsylvania president A. J. Cassatt returned from a visit to the Orleans Railway in Paris in 1901 fully confident that underwater tunnels were practical, and an electric locomotive to power the trains was feasible. That same year a board was appointed to investigate matters in detail. Among the membership was Charles W. Jacobs, whom we saw earlier, and George Gibbs, the man who would be to PRR electrification work what George Washington was to the Revolutionary War. Samuel Rea, a Pennsy vice-president and early advocate of both electric power and a trans-Hudson link, headed up the study team. Management continually encouraged the effort with repeated admonitions that money was to be no limiting factor in the project's design. The advice was heeded.

The Tunnel Plan

The scope and magnitude of the final proposal was breathtaking. The team ruled in favor of a direct Jersey–Manhattan crossing, rather than any roundabout plan. This was not to be a *mere* trans-Hudson route but a railway project that would be the most costly and dramatic endeavor undertaken by American industry up to the time. Its final price was $116 million when the project was finished in 1910. The original New York subway of 1904 cost but $38 million, and even William McAdoo's multifaceted Hudson Tubes, including the twin Hudson Terminal towers, were many millions below the cost of the Pennsylvania's project.

Six—and maybe seven—major phases can be identified in the project initially, and these quickly led to two more. Here are the components: 1) a five-mile two-track line would connect with the existing Pennsylvania main line east of Newark and cut across the Jersey Meadows on a high-line embankment; 2) a pair of tunnels would burrow beneath the Jersey Palisades and the Hudson River giving the road its long-sought entry into Manhattan; 3) a positively superlative terminal edifice would be constructed on the west side of Manhattan at Thirty-third Street and Seventh Avenue; 4) a four-track "subway" would tunnel crosstown from the terminal—two tracks under Thirty-second Street and two under Thirty-third Street—to the East River and continue below this body of water to Long Island City; 5) here a major storage and repair yard would be built, a facility which became known as Sunnyside Yard and encompassed seventy-five acres, providing room for 1550 passenger cars; 6) the entire project would be electrified with a 650-volt direct current over-riding third rail, and an electric locomotive would be designed that could haul the railroad's heaviest trains through the tunnels. The seventh component, if it be considered separately, was the interchange point between steam and electricity out in the Jersey Meadows, a place called Manhattan Transfer.

This was all the first phase of the Pennsy project. The second included a connection with the New York, New Haven and Hartford Railroad by means of a bridge from Long Island City across Hell Gate to the Bronx. The bridge opened in 1917, enabling through trains from the south and west to gain access to New England.* Additionally, a pair of bayside facilities at Greenville, N.J., and Bay Ridge on Long Island allowed freight cars to move from the PRR on into New England after being floated across Upper New York Bay on barges.

One additional development which gave the enterprise some measure of its extraordinary dimension was the acquisition by the Pennsylvania of the Long Island Rail Road in 1900. This once independent line, which served the growing communities to the east of New York, had begun in the 1880's to cast an eye on the East River water barrier which kept its passengers from direct access to Manhattan. The railroad did in fact develop interchanges with the Brooklyn Rapid Transit Company, and between 1898 and 1917 through service was operated between Long Island points and the BRT's elevated routes to Manhattan over the Brooklyn

---

* Through passenger cars from Boston to Washington were previously conveyed between PRR at Jersey City and the New Haven R R at Mott Haven aboard a transfer steamer. The service was inaugurated back in 1876 with the 1093-ton steamer *Maryland*, a vessel that could carry up to eight passenger cars at one time.

LIRR's first m.u. cars were these 51-foot "Gibbs cars" (MP-41) designed by Pennsy's George Gibbs to operate also in the narrow confines of the Interborough. But the railroad-subway hookup never transpired. (Author photo)

and Williamsburg bridges. But the LIRR's purchase by the Pennsylvania enabled it to be included in the New York Terminal plan, and the four-track tunnel under the East River was built for the Long Island's suburban service as much as for Pennsylvania trains enroute to Sunnyside Yards.

The LIRR began to lay dc third rail for electrified suburban service in 1905, and George Gibbs designed a smallish 51-foot multiple-unit car for the line that was very similar to a car Gibbs had earlier designed for August Belmont's Interborough Rapid Transit. The units were designated the MP-41 fleet, for which 134 cars were built. In later years the LIRR would adopt PRR's larger MP-54 design for its multiple-unit suburban fleet, and the company eventually went on to operate as wide a variety of third rail electric cars as this country has ever seen.*

The design and construction of a suitable electric passenger locomotive is itself a tale of incredible achievement by the Pennsylvania RR and Westinghouse, since the very idea of hauling a main line railroad train behind electric power was a concept scarcely nine years old in America. In 1895 the B&O electrified its Mount Royal Tunnel in Baltimore, the nation's first main line railroad electrification project, and, though the notion was rapidly catching on all over the country and the world, it still did not represent tried and true technology.

The end product of PRR's efforts was something called the DD-1. Essentially it was a pair of box cab units semi-permanently coupled back-to-back; each unit was equipped with four pilot wheels and two sets of drivers. In steam engine parlance this was a "4-4-0" classification, labeled the "D class" on the PRR. Hence two "D" locomotives became the "double D" engines, with the numeral indicating the DD-1 was the first fleet of such machines.

---
* The Pennsylvania and its subsidiaries classified passenger coaches with the letter P, followed by a numeral—P-54, P-70, and so forth. The prefix M indicates a motorized coach. Hence an MP-54 is a self-propelled version of the P-54.

Propulsion was managed in a manner which today seems quaint, if not downright outlandish. Inside each cab was mounted a large 2000 hp, *225-ton,* electric motor—"secure from snow, dirt and water." Power was transmitted to the driving wheels by a crankshaft and steam engine-like driving rods. Some observers say a DD-1, shorn of its cab shell and seen somewhat abstractly, resembles nothing as much as a side-wheel riverboat, but that's a similarity we need not force. *Scientific American* wryly noted "it is a curious instance of what might be called the vagaries of mechanical evolution that the DD-1 should be furnished with those side rods and connecting rods, the abolition of which from the electric locomotive was considered to be one of its principal points of improvement."

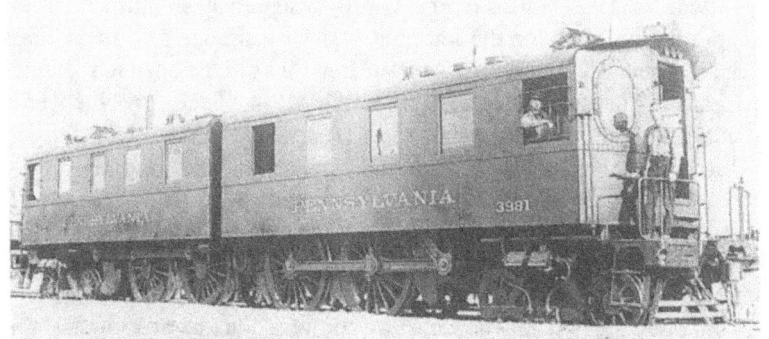

An early view of a DD-1 shows the side-rod mechanism that was used to power the distinctive electric locomotive. Contact with trackside third rail was maintained by protruding devices attached to the smaller trucks at both ends. (Smithsonian Institution)

The real point, though, is that during a series of tests conducted along third rail electrified trackage of the Pennsy-owned West Jersey and Seashore at Franklinville, N.J. in 1907, PRR engineers became convinced that axle-hung electric motors produced too much lateral sway, and so opted for the DD-1 arrangement in the interest of better balance. It was surely a wise and prudent choice, for while axle-mounted motors were later perfected to the point of acceptability and orthodoxy, the anachronistic transmission of the DD-1 served the railroad faithfully for over forty years.

The DD-1's were the most powerful locomotives ever built, had a look and a line to them that was distinctive, and can be credited with being the key element in making the entire terminal project possible. For without a dependable and effective "motor" to haul trains through the restricted confines of the tubes and tunnels, the Pennsylvania Railroad could never have been able to conquer the Hudson River. Bear in mind that the tunnels feature 1.93% grades, steeper than the road's famous line over the Allegheny Mountains, and passenger consists were regularly topping the 1000-ton mark with the introduction of all-steel equipment. Wooden passenger cars, of course, were not allowed in the underwater tunnels.

The PRR's six separate underwater tubes were built with little difficulty, and virtually none of the tragedy that plagued earlier efforts. Tunnel-building had evolved into an acceptable and almost ordinary technology, and while Sunday supplements devoted considerable copy to the a-building tubes, the project did not draw the kind of incredulous comments that were heard just a few years earlier when William Gibbs McAdoo talked about completing the unfinished Haskin tunnel.

Much was made of the multi-national background of the sandhogs, men who had worked side by side on tunnels in Egypt and South America and who would sail off after this project to some equally exotic place for their next endeavor. One article stressed the large amounts of coffee consumed by the men in the airlocks. A foreman for the contractor on the Hudson River tunnels pointed out that working under pressure increased the efficiency of his men, and consequently the company "is able to show a greater profit" from their work deep below the river bottom.

Technically the tubes were much the same as the earlier H&M project, although of larger diameter to accommodate conventional railroad trains. A plan to secure the bottom of the tunnels into the riverbed with devices called "screw piles" was eventually found to be unnecessary. Eleven iron links were needed to form each circular ring in the tube as the 194-ton Greathead Shield advanced, the record pace being 12½ feet of progress during a single eight-hour shift. A further point: the contractor on the East River tunnels was S. Pearson and Sons, the firm that tried unsuccessfully to complete the original Haskin bore several years earlier. The Hudson River crossing was under the able supervision of the O'Rourke Engineering and Construction Company. A rarely-seen plaque at midpoint of the eastbound tube, deep under the river bottom, memorializes their efforts.

The high line across the Meadows leading to the Bergen Portal on the west side of the Palisades provided some interesting engineering work. The fill used in building the elevated right-of-way was liberated from various construction projects in New York, including Penn Station itself, and transported to Jersey by barge. After crossing Newark Bay and the Hackensack River, the material was off-loaded onto railroad cars and moved into place along a temporary line built solely to facilitate construction of the final roadbed. The motive power on this project was a small steam engine rendered surplus when the Manhattan elevated lines switched to electric propulsion at the turn of the century. Once completed, *The New York Times* noted that "the embankment looks like one side of a great Chinese Wall over the great stretch of Jersey wasteland."

The thinking behind the Pennsylvania's New York terminal was that trains from the west would be serviced at Sunnyside Yard, and only minimum storage facilities were provided on Manhattan Island. For many years a large painted sign in the yard proclaimed the Sunnyside facility to be the largest passenger car yard in the world. Even today, serving a much reduced passenger volume and with many of its tracks no longer in use, Sunnyside is an impressive place. Inbound trains are routed into the yard around a large loop at the east end of the facility, and outbound schedules dip into the river tubes a few train lengths after clearing the yard. Also at Sunnyside is a complex junction so LIRR trains can go their separate ways to Jamaica and Long Island points, and in the years after 1917, New England-bound trains were able to be routed onto the Hell Gate Bridge from Sunnyside. Something even regular and observant travelers through the four-track East River tubes fail to notice is that just inside the Sunnyside portal the middle two tracks—tunnels B and C—cross over each other to insure a proper alignment of eastbound and westbound trains at both Sunnyside and Penn Station. (see diagram)

LIRR Opening Day

The PRR's East River tubes were ready for service before the Hudson crossing, and on September 8, 1910—two and a half years after McAdoo opened the H&M—trains of tuscan red multiple-unit cars lettered Long Island began running between Manhattan and various points on the LIRR's electrified zone.

Expectedly, a revised timetable was put into effect on the LIRR with the opening of the tunnels, and at 3:36 A.M. on opening day, train No. 1702, a two-car consist carrying principally baggage and newspapers, quietly slid out of the new station and under the East River bound for Winfield Junction. At 3:41 a conventional passenger train, with a motorman named W. (but not C.) Fields notching out the controller, departed from track 19 for the same destination, and at 4:30 the first inbound schedule, from Jamaica, made its landfall on Manhattan Island. Later in the morning, designated "Tunnel Day" throughout Long Island, ceremonial departures left for connections to points all over the island, and a fleet of 140 daily trains opened a new era for Queens, Nassau and Suffolk counties. *The New York Times* ventured that the project

From New Jersey, Pennsy's rails dove under the mighty Hudson through Bergen Portal, described by a contemporary as "a finely proportioned keystone." Photo was taken December 4, 1910, a week after service commenced. Today a highway overpass obstructs the view. (Smithsonian Institution)

was "the greatest thoroughfare to the eastward out of Manhattan ever devised, making easily accessible to the undeveloped insular territory beyond the river the pulsing heart of the metropolis, America's chief centre of life." The only negative notes were fears that the new tunnels would trigger such rapid growth on Long Island that needed municipal services would not be available for the soon-to-swell population.

"Tunnel Day" is romantically remembered on Long Island as a day of unrelenting revelry, but it was not quite all sweetness and light. Many objected that LIRR charged its New York passengers fourteen cents extra to ride through the tubes, compared with the older ferryboat ride across the East River from Long

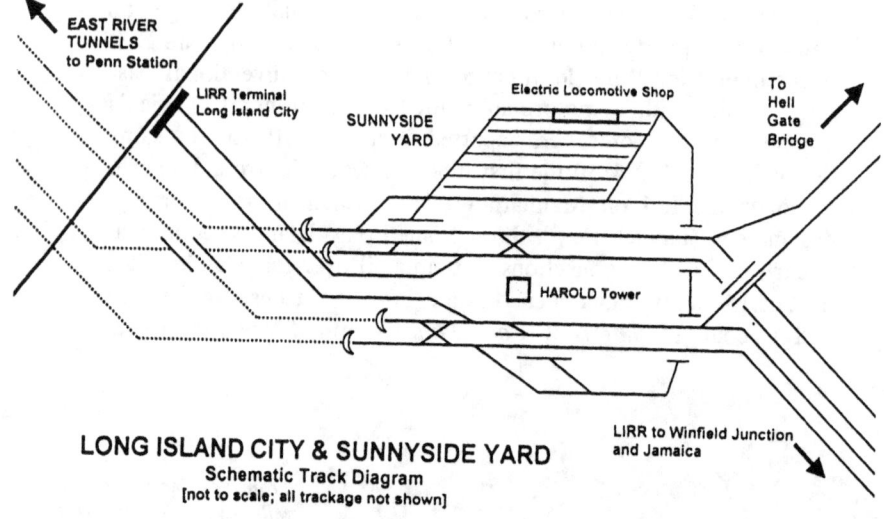

LONG ISLAND CITY & SUNNYSIDE YARD
Schematic Track Diagram
[not to scale; all trackage not shown]

Island City to the foot of Thirty-fourth Street; indeed traffic on the ferries was a robust 77% of normal on September 8, 1910.* One man on a mid-afternoon trip from Rockaway Beach wanted to pay the extra fare by check, another asked to be put off the train in the middle of the tunnel, "exactly fourteen cents away from your fancy new station," while yet a third refused to pay at all, then relented, and handed the conductor fifteen cents with the remark: "Keep the change, my contribution to the new tunnel."

On the night of Tunnel Day a banquet held at the Garden City Hotel in Nassau County commemorated the big event. Even as LIRR trains were operating into the new mid-Manhattan terminal, crews were readying the huge edifice for its full and complete opening in late November. On the very same day the Long Island was making transit history in New York, it should be noted the *London Daily Mail* awarded a cup to one John Moissant of Chicago for his successful execution of a Paris to London airplane flight. Moissant was quoted in a cable dispatch as predicting trans-Atlantic flights in five years.

---

* The LIRR continued to operate the East River ferry line until March 3, 1925, when the iron-hulled sidewheelers *Southampton* and *Pennsylvania* closed out the service.

PRR Opening Day

At 9:30 p.m. on Saturday, November 26, 1910, with William Howard Taft in the White House, Jack Johnson the heavyweight champion of the world, and the Royal Mail Steamer *Mauretania* the pride of the North Atlantic, doors were swung back, barricades removed, and the main area of Penn Station opened to the public. A person described in the press only as "a little man" raced across the concourse and purchased the first ticket to be sold in the facility—a round trip to Elizabeth, New Jersey. How anomalous that a station which would become the gateway to the nation, that would dispatch through sleeping cars to Florida, California, Canada and Mexico, sold its first ticket for a ride into the nearby suburbs.

The first train to carry passengers west out of the station and under the Hudson River departed at 12:02 a.m. on November 27, and it was a modest schedule—a local for Perth Amboy. At 12:40 a through train for the south via Washington departed. At 12:21 the telautograph in the waiting room came alive, and nine minutes later the first inbound train, *The Washington Express*, drew up to one of Penn Station's eleven platforms and unloaded passengers. At 1:00 a.m. an express left for Philadelphia, and then the station was quiet until 7:00 when service again began.

This was the first official operation of PRR's new terminal for revenue passengers. However, to insure a smooth transition the railroad actually began running empty trains between Sunnyside and Manhattan Transfer on simulated schedules two weeks before opening day. In other words, the new terminal complex was put through an extensive shakedown well in advance of the opening.

After midnight on Penn Station's opening day, PRR curtailed its ferryboat operations across the Hudson. While continuing to run its fleet of double-ended steamers out of Exchange Place for Manhattan terminals at the foot of Cortlandt Street and Desbrosses Street, the once popular line to Twenty-third Street, as well as a run to Brooklyn, were permanently abandoned. PRR suggested that Brooklyn-bound passengers could reach their destination from Penn Station by taking a special Long Island shuttle that ran through the East River tunnels, and then backtracked to the LIRR's Flatbush Avenue Terminal. Pending completion of McAdoo's New York–Newark line a year later, PRR operated shuttle trains behind steam engines from Manhattan Transfer to

ACTION AT BERGEN PORTAL. Above, train No. 59, "The Congressional," emerges from under the mighty Hudson enroute to Manhattan Transfer. It's October 11, 1914. (Smithsonian Institution)

Train No. 2, "The Pennsylvania Limited," behind a stocky L-5 dc motor heads into Bergen Portal under the newly installed ac catenary. This extra-rare photo is dated September 25, 1932. (Smithsonian Institution) Below: Forty-one years later the name of the game is "Amtrak" and the name of the train is "The National Limited," powered by GG-1 No. 900 drawing 11,000 volts ac from that same catenary. Wires duck under U.S. Route 1 overpass. (Photo by author)

Exchange Place, where the Hudson Tubes were then in operation, thus affording passengers the opportunity of arriving at any of the Manhattan locations served by the ferries or the H&M as well as, of course, the new Penn Station uptown at Thirty-third Street.

The layout of Penn Station terminal, then and now, consists in a single level of tracks—twenty-one of them. But passenger access is from separate levels of the station, so that Long Island trains, using the northernmost platforms, are boarded from what is a "lower" level of the station. Parent Pennsy's trains, departing from the southernmost platforms, are reached from the terminal's main or "upper" level. And thanks to a smartly designed system of passageways, detraining PRR passengers are fed onto the lower level, keeping them separated from outbound traffic. When the new Grand Central opened in 1913, it did in fact feature two separate and distinct levels, with separate and distinct tracks on each, and much was made of the arrangement. New Yorkers tend to confuse the two terminals, and understandably misled by the two "levels" at Penn Station, presumed that the older terminal also had two levels of tracks. But it didn't then and it doesn't now.

The new PRR terminal generated an enormous amount of local traffic in midtown Manhattan, so much so that the Metropolitan Street Railway scheduled its cars on the Thirty-fourth Street crosstown line on a hard-to-believe *twenty second* headway during rush hours. Traffic on the Sixth and Ninth Avenue els was also reported quite heavy, but PRR Vice President Sam Rea took note of a missing element in the station plan: "One important thing, however, remains undone, and that is while the company has constructed the facilities for subway connections the city has not yet produced these necessary rapid transit facilities to accommodate its own citizens and the public arriving and departing from the new station. It is a matter of deep regret that the city's subway system, with proper connections, is not complete or ready to perform their necessary function."

Anyone familiar with Penn Station today can scarcely imagine what the place must have been like without the many underground passageways linking the terminal with the city's various subway lines. In 1910 the nearest station was the H&M's Thirty-third Street terminal, a block away, and the closest point where one could catch the Interborough was either four long blocks to the east, or nine short ones to the north. It was not until 1917 that the Seventh Avenue subway was opened and direct access to Penn Station became a reality.

Exchange Place terminal was by no means abandoned with the opening of Penn Station. In the railroad's grand design, Exchange Place was to function principally as a commuter terminal, while the line's long distance trains would use the new facility, and this seemed quite sensible since the area adjacent to Penn Station had not yet become a major business and commercial district. Seven daily Philadelphia trains were also carded out of the older terminal and to discourage commuters, as well as to help recoup expenses, PRR instituted a ten-cent surcharge on tickets routed into Penn Station. And more: there was no reduced fare available for commuter tickets into the new terminal. A multiple-ride ticket that brought a man from New Brunswick to Cortlandt Street for six dollars cost twelve dollars into the uptown station.

The railroad was genuinely proud of its accomplishment. For weeks PRR ballyhooed the advent of the new terminal, and passengers were urged to call the company's New York offices—"Madison 1032"—for up-to-date information on long distance schedules. Perhaps one of the railroad's own advertisements said it best: "Capital and labor directed by genius have given New York the supreme advantage of the age." The remark is surely dated by its tone, but it stands as an apt description of the project in any event.

K4 Pacific No. 1361 sits at the bumper post in Exchange Place terminal on a May day in 1955. Two years later the 1361 was installed as a permanent exhibit alongside PRR main at Horseshoe Curve. (Author photo)

Rival Jersey Central, meanwhile, tried very hard to remain unimpressed by all the hoopla. It continued to promote its own New York–Philadelphia service with the slogan: "Hard Coal, No Smoke, No Tunnels." A similar refrain was pressed by CNJ's partner on the run, the Philadelphia and Reading: "No tunnels, nor transfer changes; Hard Coal, No Smoke."

Some negative reaction to the terminal project emanated from Philadelphia, where *The Evening Bulletin* complained that the railroad was guilty of rank discrimination, since Broad Street Station compared very poorly with the new edifice in Manhattan. Another sour note was sounded by *The Literary Digest* when, in the flush of the terminal's success, it suggested that perhaps a Hudson River bridge would have been a better alternative. "Are the Pennsylvania Tunnels a Blunder?" asked the magazine.

Change at Manhattan Transfer

The subaqueous tubes, the terminal, the wonderful DD-1. These are the obvious things about the New York Tunnel Extension, and the facets of the project that justly deserve careful exposition and detailed analysis. But in the work-a-day world of railroading, the glamour of Penn Station and the engineering marvels wrought by John Henry Greathead take a back seat to Manhattan Transfer. Manhattan Transfer was all railroad.

Manhattan Transfer was the place where the Pennsylvania's fleet of steam locomotives—noble engines that had breasted the Alleghenies and raced the wind across the flatlands of Indiana—had to be waved aside for the highly specialized finale into New York. And Manhattan Transfer was also the place where the "standard railroad of the world" shared platform space with the Hudson Tubes, according to the pact McAdoo and Cassatt reached in 1903.

Simply described, Manhattan Transfer was a pair of 28-by-1100-foot high-level platforms, connected by an underpass, and including skylighted umbrella sheds which one journalist described as "coop like." To the north was a three-track right-of-way of the Lackawanna's Morris and Essex line, to the south the brackish water of the Passaic River. The only vegetation that thrived in the swampy area were reeds and marsh grass. The facility was located beyond milepost eight on the new high line from Penn Station where the extension joined PRR's original main line from Exchange Place. As an aside, the Transfer was only about seven miles from Exchange Place. For many years mileposts along the PRR main continued to reflect distances from the older Jersey City terminal, and were not true readings from Penn Station.

McAdoo's trains emerged from their underground mole at Waldo Avenue, Jersey City, climbing over the top of the New Jersey Junction Railway and proceeding through Shanley's Cut to a spot beyond "SC Tower," where the tracks joined the PRR main line. Just past Manhattan Transfer they swung off onto a concrete and steel elevated structure, proceeded through Harrison —making a station stop there—and then across the Passaic River to a stub-end terminal at Park Place, Newark.

Hudson and Manhattan service was extended to Manhattan Transfer on October 1, 1911, and a few months later when line work was completed, trains began to operate into Park Place. A new and somewhat different fleet of cars was ordered for the Newark route by the H&M and its partner in the service; designated the MP-38 fleet, they resembled the original tunnel equipment, but featured porthole windows on the car ends and a railroad-like roof profile. The MP-38 notation was PRR practice, and although only a portion of the Newark cars were actually owned by the railroad—the rest by H&M—all were painted in Pennsy's distinctive tuscan red, contrasting to the H&M's own "black cars."

A feature of Manhattan Transfer that was extremely unusual was the fact that one could not get to the station save by rail. Although it was located at a highly inaccessible spot in the Jersey Meadows, this posed no difficulties for PRR's purposes; it was to function solely as a place for passengers to change trains and the railroad to change locomotives. Many stories are still told of fortune seekers from places like Dubuque or Duluth who long nurtured the American dream of "hitting it big" in New York City. After days of traveling they were understandably misled when a conductor stuck his head inside the coach and announced "Manhattan Transfer"—they presumed this station to be their long-sought destination, the promised land. The punch lines vary, but the stories turn on the station's complete and total lack of egress to city streets.

In addition to two tracks beside each of the platforms, there were several bypass routes (see pages 40–41). Light engines regularly used the inside tracks, and certain H&M New York–Newark trains

A three-car "McAdoo Reds" train in joint service, Jersey City to Newark. (Collection of Leo Ross)

that were not scheduled to stop at Manhattan Transfer could scoot past on outside tracks. McAdoo's cars were a foot or more narrower than conventional railroad rolling stock, and to avoid having passengers jump a wide gap to board their trains, a gantlet was installed along each of the outside tracks so both styles of equipment could use the platform with ease.

Operationally Manhattan Transfer was simple enough. When an inbound—*east bound* in PRR argot—train braked to a halt beside the platform, men jumped in behind the tender, closed the angle cocks, pulled the coupler pin, and waved the steam engine off. The road crew then moved their locomotive to nearby Meadows Yard for servicing, and, eventually, a new assignment. Once the steamer was clear, Tower S* lined up appropriate switches, semaphore arms moved into clear position, and a DD-1 backed down to couple onto the waiting train. Steam and air lines were joined, brakes tested, and after a pause of just a few minutes the train was given a highball, and with a barely perceptible clank of side rods audible above the peal of the engine's bell, moved off toward the Bergen Portal.

Meanwhile passengers heading for Exchange Place and the ferries would have gotten off for their connection, often a local from New Brunswick or the Amboys which would operate straight

---

* There were two towers—or "cabins" in PRR's then-current lingo—at Manhattan Transfer. Cabin S was at the east end of the station and Cabin N at the west end. Cabin S, now called Hudson Tower, still stands, virtually the last remnant of Manhattan Transfer.

Manhattan Transfer. You are facing east on the south platform at a quiet moment in June of 1912. (Collection of Leo Ross)

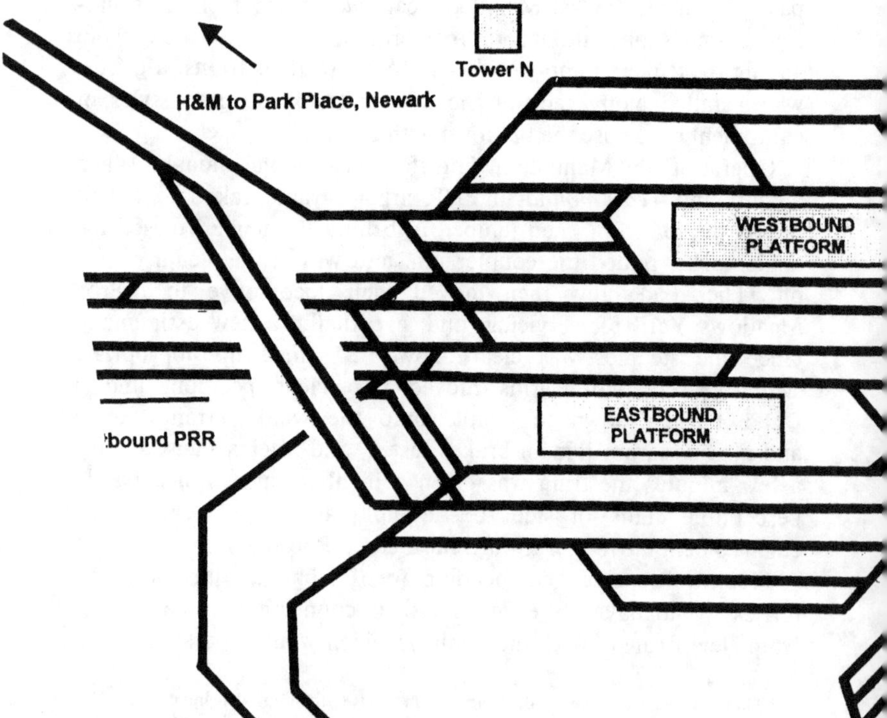

LARGEST FLEET OF AIR-CONDITIONED TRAINS IN T

New York, Philadelphia and Washington to Indianapolis, Loui

		Express	The Metropolitan	The Metropolitan	The Fort Dearborn	The Liberty Limited	"Spirit of St. Louis"	The American
For stations between Pittsburgh and Xenia consult pages 13 and 14.				25-155 -109			★	★
For Sleeping, Parlor and Dining Cars see pages 27 to 34.		13	25-155		75-27	59-31	31	65
		Daily	Daily	Daily	Daily	Daily	Daily	Daily
		P M	A M	A M	NOON	P M	A M	NOON
	Lv. Boston, Mass. ▼ (N. Y., N. H. & H.)	8 00	...	...	...	...	9 00	12 00
	Ar. New York, N. Y. (Penna. Station)	2 10	...	...	...	...	2 15	5 15
.0	Lv. New York, N. Y. (Pa. Sta.)—(E. S. T.)	2 30	8 00	8 00	12 00	...	3 40	6 10
	Lv. New York, N. Y. (Hudson Terminal)	2 00	7 50	7 50	11 50	...	u 3 30	6 00
	Jersey City, N. J. (Exchange Place)	u 2 03	u 7 53	u 7 53	u11 53	...	u 3 33	u 6 03
	Ar. Manhattan Transfer, N. J. (v)	2 17	8 07	8 07	12 07	...	3 47	6 17
	Lv. Manhattan Transfer, N. J. (v)	2 43	8 13	8 13	12 13	...	3 53	6 23
10.1	Newark, N. J. (Market Street)	2 47	8 17	8 17	12 17	...	3 57	6 27
48.3	Princeton Junction, N. J.	...	...	...	...	...	...	t 7 06
58.0	Trenton, N. J.	...	9 06	9 06	1 09	...	...	...
.0	Lv. Atlantic City, N. J. (See page 37.)	...	...	...	...	...	...	...
	Lv. Philadelphia, Pa.							
85.8	North Philadelphia (Note A)	4 12	9 36	9 36	1 39	...	5 12	7 46
91.3	Broad Street Station	...	10 07	10 07	2 10	...	...	...
	Pennsylvania Station (30th Street)	...	10 11	10 11	2 14	...	...	...
111.3	Paoli, Pa.	4 42	10 41	10 41	2 45	...	5 41	8 16
150.4	Lancaster, Pa.	5 47	11 38	11 38	3 48	...	6 41	9 17
195.3	Ar. Harrisburg, Pa.	6 31	12 20	12 20	4 32	...	7 24	9 59

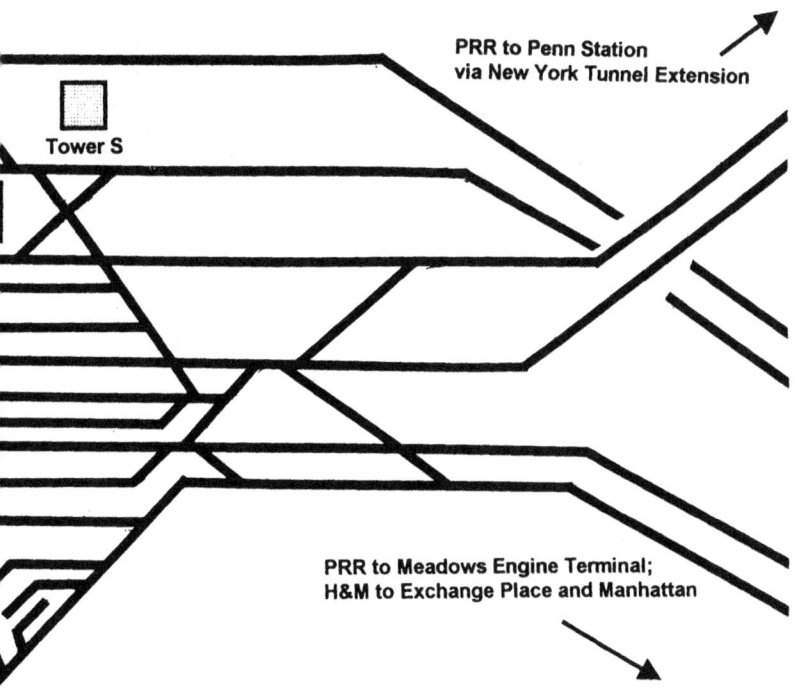

MANHATTAN TRANSFER
Schematic Track Diagram
[not to scale; all trackage not shown]

Out from Penn Station, DD-1 No. 24 pauses at Manhattan Transfer to allow a steam engine to take over on a westbound schedule. Below, westbound motor in motion after the cut-off to make way for steam power. Picture also shows gantlet track arrangement that enabled narrower H&M rolling stock to board passengers without the hazard of a gap between cars and platform. (Both photos from Harry P. Albrecht)

Lower photo: With body shell removed, the primitive muscle of a DD-1 is revealed. Powerful, low-r.p.m. electric motors transmit energy to driving wheels via counter-weighted rods. (Smithsonian Institution)

through to Jersey City behind steam. Others would board a tuscan red MP-38, and arrive in New York via Hudson Terminal.

To provide greater flexibility, PRR at one time even worked up shuttle service into Penn Station for passengers on Exchange Place-bound trains. The road outfitted six P-54 suburban coaches and two combines with dc traction motors and ran them over the new third rail line. This service did not last beyond 1922, however, and the cars were then transferred to the Long Island and absorbed in that road's growing fleet of MP-54 units.

With all the trains coming and going at the Transfer a workable system was needed to identify which trains were headed where. Suspended from the platform roof was a set of large boxes; and inside each box were twenty or so signs, lettered for appropriate "name" trains, as well as common destinations. These signs were pivoted, and prior to the arrival of any train, a platform attendant would come by and lower the correct sign with a long pole, semaphore-like. A similar system was also installed at the LIRR's Jamaica Station, as well as Pennsy's Thirtieth Street Station in Philadelphia, where they kept travelers informed for many years. After Manhattan Transfer closed, the sign boxes there were moved into the new station in Newark. There they served until the late 1960s, when a new system was developed.

During its years, Manhattan Transfer dispatched some of the finest steam locomotives ever to run under the Pennsy house flag. In 1910, when the Transfer came on line, the road was experimenting with various designs of E class Atlantics—4-4-2 types—an evolution which would culminate in the E-6s of 1913, a locomotive that became a classic of rare proportion in the ranks of U.S. steam power, and that is fittingly memorialized in Frederick Westing's book *Apex of the Atlantics*. But even the E-6s was to be outdone. In May 1914, Juniata Shops turned out No. 1737, a Pacific-type locomotive that the road designated the K-4s. The K-4s was built in quantity between 1917 and 1928, the fleet eventually numbered 425 units, and it will ever be remembered as the epitome of steam power on the Pennsylvania Railroad. While Manhattan Transfer saw many of PRR's famous D-16 class 4-4-0 American-types in its early years, the E-6s and the K-4s were *the* basic steam locomotives that would be waiting at Manhattan Transfer to take over from DD-1's on westbound schedules.

A retired insurance salesman whose work often took him from New York to Wilmington and Baltimore in the 1930s and '40s tells this story: "I'd always go out to Manhattan Transfer on the tubes an hour or so before my train, because I liked getting a chance to watch the steamers. I wouldn't always get as good a seat as if I had gone uptown to Penn Station, but it was worth it to see the K-4s up close. When the engine assigned to my train came down from the yard, moved slowly through the station to wait for the connection out from the tunnel, you just knew this was the most important thing that was happening in the whole world."

Others say nightfall created a special magic at the Transfer, especially in the wintertime when the evening commuter rush took place after dark. Clusters of passengers would knot about on the platform under the yellowish glare of light bulbs, changing from the H&M to a North Jersey Coast train, or from a train out of Exchange Place to a Philadelphia "clocker." West of the station waiting K-4s and E-6s engines would signal their impatience as safety valves let loose, filling the night air with superheated steam; then in turn each of the locomotives would back down out of the darkness to take charge of a westbound train, and thunder off along the Pennsy main to Washington, or Chicago, or St. Louis, the sound of its powerful exhaust drifting easily back to the platform as the engineer moved his charge through Newark.

Railroad statisticians estimate 230 million revenue passengers used Manhattan Transfer during its lifetime. The adjective usually employed to describe the place was "drab"; in later years the red brick platforms became worn and developed a series of permanent waves. But Manhattan Transfer, for all its lack of amenities and glamour in the ordinary sense, worked its way into America's innocent years and became a genuine national institution. Perhaps it was the magic vista of the New York skyline off in the distance; maybe it was the odd-ball situation of a station with no entrance or exit. But whatever the reason, it is curious that the most colorful and best remembered locale where the DD-1 performed was not the carefully engineered tunnels, or even regal Penn Station, but a set of ordinary railroad platforms out in the middle of the Jersey Meadows.

It was John Dos Passos who gave the station its most enduring memorial when in 1925 he published a novel entitled, simply, *Manhattan Transfer*. Not that the book is *about* Manhattan Transfer in any extended sense; it's about people—people whose daily lives are entwined in all facets of New York in the 1920s. And what was more appropriate for a novel's title than the transfer point from whence so many get their first—or last—glimpse of the city?

"They had to change at Manhattan Transfer. The thumb of Ellen's new kid glove had split and she kept rubbing it nervously with her forefinger. John wore a belted raincoat and a pinkish grey hat. When he turned to her and smiled she couldn't help pulling her eyes away and staring out at the long rain that shimmered over the tracks.

" 'Here we are Ellen dear. Oh prince's daughter, you see we get the train that comes from Penn Station . . . It's funny this waiting in the wilds of New Jersey this way.' They got into the parlor car."

Ellen Thatcher, just hours after becoming the bride of John Oglethorpe, boarded an Atlantic City-bound train with her new husband. "The wheels rumbled in her head saying Man-hattan Transfer. Man-hattan Transfer."

ALTERNATING CURRENT

Less than five years after Manhattan Transfer opened, the Pennsylvania began to dabble in a new and different form of railway electrification, a technology which would alter the character of the colorful transfer point in the Jersey Meadows, and eventually be instrumental in its demise.

On March 12, 1913, then-President Rea announced that the PRR's board of directors had voted to spend $4 million to electrify suburban service out of Philadelphia. Rather than the 650 volts of direct current that the DD-1's drew from trackside third rail, a system of 11,000 volt alternating current distributed from an overhead catenary was selected. Why the change?

True enough, the Pennsylvania was more than anxious to improve the calibre of suburban operations in and around the city it still regarded as "home." Prior to electrification, Broad Street Station's sixteen stub-end tracks were hopelessly clogged by the numerous switching movements necessary with locomotive-drawn trains. The substitution of locomotive-less and bi-directional multiple-unit cars allowed a more sensible pattern of ulilization to be realized. There were other obvious advantages to electrification as well, but PRR was looking beyond the suburbs of Philadelphia on this project. It was looking to the grades of the Allegheny Mountains, and the long haul up to Gallitzin, Pa., which stood like a glacial barrier astride the line's vital east–west main.

650 volts dc. "Chairs" mounted on extra-long ties support third rail. (Author photo)

11,000 volts ac. Spidery overhead wires feed curr< to Pennsy P-5 and GG-1 locos. (Author)

Economy literally went up in smoke as helper engines had to be coupled to both the front and rear of trains assaulting the divide. If electrification could conquer the Hudson, reasoned the Pennsylvania, why not the Alleghenies?

The rub was that direct current, while tried and true as a source of power for modest-sized electrification projects, did not have good properties for transmission over long distances. Indeed in most installations, even city subway and elevated lines, electricity was generated and transmitted as alternating current and only converted to dc at lineside substations strung out along the route. While PRR was willing to stand the expense of the Philadelphia electrification for the sake of suburban services alone, its choice of an ac system clearly indicated the road had designs beyond the commutation zone, and the company itself said as much with no equivocation. But ac was not the known quantity that dc was; hence a modest experiment, looking ahead to later expansion.

On the morning of September 11, 1915, the 5:55 A.M. train from Paoli to Broad Street became the first revenue operation on the new network.* As was done earlier in designing dc electric

---

* The Paoli Local has become a celebrity of distinguished proportions in the usually glamorless world of suburban railroading. Christopher Morley extolled its charm in verse, and the service is regarded as an important cultural institution in the Philadelphia suburbs.

cars for both the Long Island and the lesser known West Jersey and Seashore, PRR turned to its own passenger car roster and selected the seventy-five-ton, sixty-four-foot P-54 suburban coach as the basic vehicle for ac service. This was not exactly a random selection; the P-54 was originally developed with the idea of an electrical retrofit very much in mind.

Initially ninety-three cars were rigged for multiple-unit service at Altoona. Each was equipped with one power truck and one trailer. Two 168-kw Westinghouse single phase "repulsion starting" motors provided pull, and a single pantograph was mounted on the motor end of the car. Catenary voltage was stepped down to an 850-volt maximum by an on-board transformer, the cooling vents for which were visible on one side of the car. The MP-54 became a true perennial on the Pennsylvania, and the fleet would eventually number just shy of five-hundred units. Most were of an all-coach configuration, but there were some combines, full baggage cars, and even RPO models, all neatly categorized in appropriate sub-classes.

Two years after electric service began to Paoli, a monster-like ac freight motor—FF-1 class No. 3931—arrived in the electrified zone to haul tonnage. "Big Liz," as the experimental engine was called, was not an outstanding success, but the principle of ac electrification was, although expansion went not westward toward the mountains but north and south along the Atlantic Coast. By 1933 wires had been stretched all the way to Exchange Place and Penn Station. At 9:00 A.M. on the morning of January 16 a bugler from New York's Sixteenth Infantry sounded "stand by": Mayor O'Brien then snipped a ceremonial ribbon, and as the bugler broke into "forward," and then "double time," the first ac-powered schedule—train no. 207 with a box-cab P-5a-class locomotive on the head end—eased out of Penn Station, through the tunnel, across the high line to Manhattan Transfer, and all the way to Philadelphia—with no change of engine. By February 1st, all forty-four New York–Philadelphia trains were fully electrified, and in the weeks that followed, ac motors were gradually assigned to all trains departing New York. To the south, the wires reached as far as Wilmington, and to the west, Paoli.*

---

* PRR's ac electrification was compatible with an earlier system installed on the New York, New Haven and Hartford RR between New York and New Haven. Consequently, after 1933 NH electric locomotives operating over the Hell Gate Bridge were able to continue under the new catenary and through the tunnels to Penn Station. DD-1's were then relieved of the assignment of forwarding New Haven trains under the East River from Sunnyside, one of their lesser-known responsibilities.

Electrified service with alternating current was also extended into the old Exchange Place terminal in Jersey City. On December 8, 1932, the 6:12 A.M. train from New Brunswick to the ferry slip signaled the start of the new order. And long before the novelty had even begun to wear off the ac system, the Pennsylvania Railroad introduced a new locomotive on its electrified lines. It was designated the GG-1, the fleet eventually numbered 139 units, and partisans insist it is the finest piece of railway equipment that has ever been built—anywhere, anytime, by anybody.

The veteran DD-1 was retired from PRR service with the advent of the ac network, as were a small fleet of L5-class dc motors the railroad ordered in 1924 to supplement the original locomotives. These elongated steeplecab machines were not very successful, but they must be mentioned as surely the strangest looking motors ever to draw amps on the Pennsylvania. Their profile would have seemed more at home hauling freight through the Swiss Alps than passengers across the Secaucus marshes.

Twenty-three of the DD-1's were transferred to the Long Island, and they served into the 1950s moving that line's trains between Penn Station and Jamaica, where they gave way to steam —and later diesel—power for the continuation along one of the LIRR's non-electrified branches, the very same style of service for which they were designed. DD-1's returned to the limelight briefly during the 1939–40 New York World's Fair, when several crack Pennsylvania trains operated directly to the fair grounds in Flushing over LIRR's third rail trackage behind the veteran motors.

The third rail was removed from the Tunnel Extension out to Manhattan Transfer, but it was retained inside the Hudson River tunnels themselves, and into the 1970s a single DD-1 remained on the active roster to haul the "wire train," a work extra which kept the ac catenary in repair, and which drew dc from the third rail, thus allowing the overhead to be de-energized in the interest of safety. In 1970 this final DD-1 was fittingly retired, and it now resides in the Pennsylvania State Museum at Strasburg, its place on the "wire train" having been taken by a slightly younger ex-New York Central "T" motor, a veteran of electric service out of Grand Central. Such a maneuver, of course, could never have occurred had not the Penn Central merger been consummated in 1968, and previously unthinkable corporate flexibilities become commonplace.

Even with the ac power, Manhattan Transfer continued to serve as a railroad-transit junction point, although much of the old-time charm was lost with the phase-out of the power change ritual. With the opening of a new $20 million railroad depot in Newark in June of 1937, connections were more appropriately handled there and Manhattan Transfer was closed. The H&M also abandoned service to the Park Place terminal at the same time.

Manhattan Transfer was phased out in the early hours of Sunday, June 20. On Saturday the 19th the Associated Press office in New York moved a story on its wire that began: "Manhattan Transfer, the elongated island of brick, concrete and steel in the Jersey Meadows from which incoming fortune seekers first glimpsed the fabled towers of Manhattan, passed into limbo today."

Maybe it was just a slow day for news; and then maybe it was because Manhattan Transfer was, well, because it was just special, somehow. But the fact is that newspapers in cities like Altoona and Indianapolis picked up the story and ran it in their weekend editions, and the closing of Manhattan Transfer was given more extensive press coverage outside New York than was the opening of Penn Station and the tunnels in 1910.

The platforms were quickly demolished, though from 1937 through the late 1960s, it was relatively easy to pick out the spot where they stood from a passing **PRR** or **H&M** train. In 1967 the Aldene Plan was implemented, and the Jersey Central Railroad began to operate its trains into PRR's Newark Station. To store

PRR's fleet of DD-1 electric locomotives continued to haul trains for the PRR-owned Long Island Railroad after their days with the parent road, but eventually all DD-1's, save one, were sent to the scrap heap. The sole survivor is this unit which has been preserved at the Railroad Museum of Pennsylvania, in Strasburg. Each of a DD-1's two units was assigned its own road number and the preserved set includes No. 3936 and No. 3937. In practice, a pair of DD-1's were identified by a simplified two-digit number.

equipment between runs, a yard was built to the south of, and partly on the site of Manhattan Transfer. A keen eye can still pick out where the westbound platform stood.

Exchange Place station was abandoned outright in 1961, and soon afterward torn down. In later years it no longer functioned as *the* commuter alternative to Penn Station, and merely handled a decreasing number of suburban trains whose passengers were able to change for the H&M at Newark anyway. The ferry service, for instance, which had been reduced to only two boats on a half-hour schedule between Exchange Place and Cortlandt Street by the end of World War II, was discontinued entirely in 1950, the Pennsylvania being the first of the five railroads which operated ferry connections to go completely out of that business. And the fine old steel arch trainshed was demolished even earlier and became part of the wartime scrap drive.

One last hurrah which Exchange Place managed, though, took place in the late 1950s as steam locomotives were rapidly disappearing from U.S. railroads. The Pennsylvania's plan for dieselization called for certain non-electrified lines in New Jersey to be the final stamping grounds for steam. As late as 1957, Exchange Place was still dispatching a K-4s-powered schedule each day to Bay Head Junction down the North Jersey Coast. To make it even more appropriate, locomotives were serviced between runs at Meadows engine terminal. And the final touch is that despite over forty-five years of electrification, the last year of steam power on Pennsylvania passenger trains saw K-4s locomotives operating through and past the site of Manhattan Transfer.

A train of PRR MP-54 multiple-unit cars pauses to board passengers at the 1937-built station in Newark, the facility that replaced Manhattan Transfer.

Part Three: TRANSITION

THE HUDSON & MANHATTAN reached full maturity, actually, with the opening of the Newark service in 1911. The line's original one-track repair shop at Hoboken was superseded by a large permanent facility at Henderson Street, Jersey City, just east of the Grove Street station. A peculiarity of the original installation was that cars had to be hoisted out of the tubes, one at a time, aboard a 100,000-pound-capacity elevator to gain access to the temporary ground-level service area. The elevator, incidentally, which was used to deliver all the H&M's new rolling stock in 1908, remained in operation for many years and was often used by flat cars ferrying supplies to maintenance projects.

Yet another aspect of the old H&M was its electrical generating equipment. A company-owned powerhouse on Washington Street in Jersey City was outfitted with four Curtis vertical steam turbines, two rated at 6000 kw and two at 3000 kw. In keeping with what would eventually become a near universal trend in rapid transit, the H&M eventually sold off its powerhouse. Since the mid-1920s, the line has purchased its electricity. New York's Con Edison supplies current as far as Journal Square, while Jersey-based Public Service handles the line beyond to Newark.

Riding statistics on the line improved steadily year after year. In 1914, just shy of 60 million were carried, and the line's car fleet numbered 226 steel motor cars. In 1927 the passenger count reached an all-time high of 113 million; then the Holland Tunnel for automobiles opened and the picture starts to get cloudy. In 1928 the line took delivery of twenty-eight new cars, the last it would order for thirty years. Even before this, unfavorable signs were there to be seen by the farsighted. On February 28, 1920, acting transit commissioner Daniel L. Ryan of New York turned down the line's request for an extension of its still-pending franchise rights to build beyond Thirty-third Street to Grand Central. This was the H&M's seventeenth request for a continuance of its option; the decision meant that the original terminal at Thirty-third Street would remain the northern limit of the line's spearhead into midtown Manhattan. Needless to say the H&M never did become a serious contender for operating any part of the $300 million subway network the City of New York let out for contract in 1913, and such proposals as four-tracking the downtown tunnels* and running a line south to a connection with the Jersey Central Railroad, perhaps even to Staten Island, never got beyond the talking stage.

Bad Days on the H&M

In post-war years the Hudson Tubes fell upon evil days. Deficits mounted, ridership dropped from the 1927 high of 113 million to a 1958 low of just over 26 million, and in 1954 the line entered receivership, never to emerge. Most financial analysts felt that only rental income from Hudson Terminal prevented such a fate from coming to pass many years earlier.

One of the court-appointed trustees was Herman T. Stichman; in the years following bankruptcy, Stichman was able to make credible efforts toward re-organization of the company. In July of 1958 the line put into service the first cars of an order of fifty that would replace all the MP-38's on the Newark line. The cars, manufactured in St. Louis, were the nation's first production-model air-conditioned transit cars, though they otherwise resembled post-war equipment in Boston and Cleveland. Nevertheless, when somebody realized that 1958 also marked the H&M line's golden jubilee, the arrival of the new equipment was celebrated in due and proper course. Among the promotional gimmicks tried as part of the anniversary was the revival of an earlier McAdoo idea—a car reserved for women only. It was just as unsuccessful in 1958 as it had been in 1908.

Stichman was able to win generous tax relief from several of the line's jurisdictions, but over the long haul the efforts, while noble, proved insufficient, and prospects for the future grew dim. Many called for an assumption of the service by the fiscally sound Port of New York Authority, Stichman making the wholly reasonable

---

* Not really "four-tracking" but building an additional set of tubes from Hudson Terminal that would have made their Jersey landfall near Erie Terminal. The track layout at Hudson Terminal was built in anticipation of this.

After the Port Authority took over the H&M in 1962, PATH used the old railroad's equipment until newly-designed PA-class cars were available. Car No. 256, the last of the "black cars," was donated by PATH to the National Museum of Transport, in St. Louis." (Port Authority of New York and New Jersey)

point that it was the PA's automobile tunnels that served to drive away (no pun), large chunks of the H&M line's ridership. But the Port Authority had long expressed disinterest in undertaking any money-losing rail ventures, and seemed unlikely to change its mind. Prophets of doom began to predict the line's total demise. Suggestions for non-rail use of the tunnels included such delightful absurdities as an underground mushroom farm, enabling Manhattan restaurants to garnish their sirloins with fresh produce.

The Recovery

Then in 1962 the improbable happened. The nation was slowly awakening to the fact that the automobile was no total answer to urban transport problems, and, yes, the Port Authority would be willing to buy out *and operate* the bankrupt railway. In a separate but parallel development, the Port Authority would repeat the H&M's own experience of 1908. On the site of the line's by then deteriorating Hudson Terminal it planned to erect two massive office buildings to be called the World Trade Center. The 110-story towers would be the world's tallest buildings, just to underscore the scope of the Authority's proposal and give some hint of the rents a landlord might expect to collect on the first of each month. When completed in the mid-1970's, the two buildings had cost the Port Authority $900 million.

There was some slight haggling over price, but not much, really, all considered, and after appropriate state legislation was passed by both New York and New Jersey, a Port Authority subsidiary, the Port Authority Trans-Hudson Corporation (PATH) came into existence. On September 1, 1962, the new agency assumed responsibility for the former McAdoo tubes. The takeover was nearly derailed when the New York Appellate Court ruled the deal unconstitutional in February of 1963, but this decision was quickly reversed on appeal, and the U.S. Supreme Court dismissed further appeals in November of '63.

Equipment replacement became a very important priority for the new operators. In 1965 the first of a gloriously modern fleet of new cars arrived on the property from the St. Louis Car Division of General Steel Industries. Initially, 160 of what are called the "PA class" cars were delivered. Unusual in that they come in

Storage yards and turnback facilities west of Journal Square station. PA cars, "black cars" (in yellow paint disguise) and Class K rolling stock are in evidence. (Author photo)

two different body styles—cab-less "C" cars and cab-equipped "A" cars—and finished off in metallic silver-blue and stainless steel, they could hardly have been more colorful and futuristic looking. Many transit observers say they are the epitome of contemporary design, even though they lack the exotic automatic controls that were then appearing on new transit lines such as Lindenwold line in southern New Jersey and the BART system in the San Francisco area.

An interesting footnote to the PA cars is that prior to entering service three of them were coupled behind a Pennsylvania GG-1 and hauled over to the Long Island's electrified trackage for high-speed testing. What makes this doubly interesting is that it repeats an earlier experience: the H&M's original equipment ran shakedown trials on the Second Avenue El in Manhattan in 1908.*

H&M's K class cars of 1958 would remain in service under PATH auspices, their once-gray car bodies repainted blue and silver to match the new PA's. Together, the K class and the new PATH equipment managed to replace all pre-war rolling stock from the H&M era, although some older "black cars" survived as maintenance equipment for a number of years and could be found at various points along the system painted an unlikely shade of bright yellow.

A further note on the K class: When purchased, twenty cars were owned by, and lettered for, the Hudson & Manhattan, while thirty were the property of the Pennsylvania and designated class MP-52 by the railroad. After the PATH takeover, the railroad withdrew from active partnership in the New York–Newark service, and the thirty cars—actually twenty-seven due to accident loss—were leased to PATH for a dollar a year. Following this transaction the entire class of cars was generally identified as the K class and the MP-52 designation was dropped.

A fast inspection of H&M properties by PATH revealed a sorry history of deferred maintenance in such vital areas as electrical power distribution, maintenance equipment and the automatic signal system. Consequently, to insure effective operation, PATH has spent $250 million in capital improvements between 1962 and 1974 to bring the entire system into a dependable, trouble-free state.

Work was quickly begun on the massive World Trade Center, and Hudson Terminal fell to the wrecker's ball. In July of 1971

---

*One point of difference: in 1965 the LIRR main was festooned with happy traction buffs recording the event on film, while in 1908 the strange new cars that appeared on the El were a puzzlement to all, including the press.

PATH trains began operating into and out of a new terminal at the site, one with platforms to accommodate longer trains, this being the best way to increase rush-hour capacity on a system that operates perilously close to absolute capacity when the commuters are out in force. The new terminal is also the nation's first air-conditioned subway station, continuing the pioneer tradition of the H&M.

The original Hudson Terminal, while outmoded and in need of replacement, was a colorful place and should not be banished from mind. It could be said to have resembled more an old-fashioned trolley terminal than a subway depot. It featured a five-track loop, like its replacement, but the curves were much sharper and trains screeched to high heaven as wheel flanges heeled into the approach tracks. During the course of the World Trade

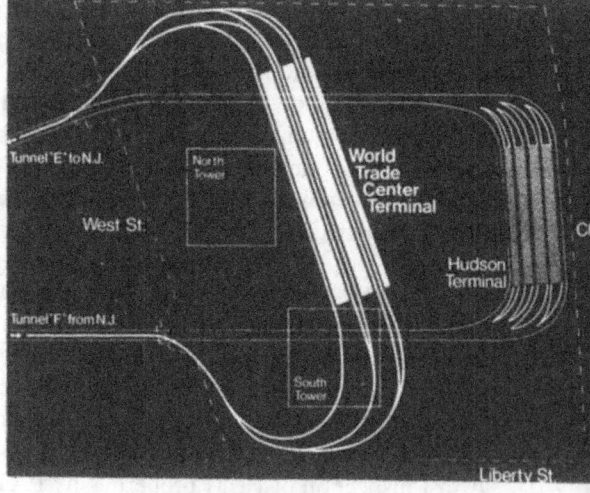

Where H&M car wheels squealed through the curves into trolley-style Hudson Terminal, PA-equipped trains later rolled in air-conditioned comfort. (PATH diagram)

Center's construction, the tube approach to Hudson Terminal was exhumed for a length, and in a very unusual engineering feat continued to be used by trains while suspended in mid-air by temporary shoring. This was in the excavation west of the original terminal, and it is here that the new station has been built, below the grade of the original route, and six stories below street level.

A complementary development to the World Trade Center was the construction of a new multimillion-dollar terminal and area redevelopment effort at Journal Square in Jersey City, a project that upgraded the old H&M station there to improve overall rail operations and provide a broader range of amenities for PATH passengers.

The Aldene Plan

On April 30, 1967, the so-called Aldene Plan to consolidate and merge Jersey commuter services went into effect, and PATH took on further responsibilities. The Central Railroad Company of New Jersey closed down its tidewater passenger depot in Jersey City, discontinued its ferry boats,* and began to operate its entire fleet of passenger trains into Newark's Pennsylvania Station. PATH then became a principal link for passengers to Manhattan, and in late 1967 the Erie Lackawanna RR abandoned its Hudson River ferries—essentially the successor to the 1775 Hoboken Ferry—and the tubes realized a long-ago dream of William Gibbs McAdoo. For in 1908 when the tunnels were first opened, McAdoo felt they would provide effective replacement for *all* Hudson River ferryboats, and suggested that if trans-Hudson

With the implementation of the Aldene Plan in 1967, Jersey Central trains abandoned their riverside terminal in Jersey City and began to operate out of the one-time PRR facility in Newark. The year is 1973 and CNJ diesel locomotive No. 3683 is moving its train from a storage yard adjacent to the site of Manhattan Transfer into Newark where it will board passengers, while a PATH schedule from the World Trade Center prepares to make a quick stop at Harrison.

passengers took the H&M, the time saved by passengers in twelve months would amount to nine hundred years. But what didn't happen in 1908 did come to pass fifty-nine years later. Shortly after 6:00 P.M. on Wednesday, November 23, 1967, Captain Cornelius Steeval rang up "finished with engines" on EL's 1460-ton steam double-ender *Elmira*—a vessel that was built three years *before* the H&M operated its very first train—and the long

---

* The very last ferry trip was made in the early morning hours of Sunday, April 30, but the vessel was *The Tides*, one of two diesel-powered boats the railroad had borrowed during its final years. On Friday, April 28, at 5:45 P.M., the final crossing was made by the last of CNJ's own fleet, steam-powered *Elizabeth*.

Speeding east across the Jersey meadows, a Hudson Terminal-bound train of K class cars. PRR insignia on lead car in this 1959 view is indicative of "joint service" arrangement.

Opposite: A Newark-bound train has just crossed the Hackensack River. This trackage is now used exclusively by PATH although it was once the H&M-PRR "joint service" area. (Both photos by author)

and colorful history of Hudson River ferries came to a sad and irrevocable end. Just to keep the record straight it should be mentioned that while *Elmira* made the celebrated and perhaps official last run, *Lackawanna* actually squeezed in a post-finale crossing several minutes later to close out the service and a 192-year tradition. *Lackawanna,* incidentally, was built in 1891 and served on the Hoboken Ferry for seventy-six years.

Implementation of the Aldene Plan also meant that PATH needed more cars, and in 1967 forty-four additional PA units arrived on the property from St. Louis. PATH also streamlined the old H&M fare structure. From time immemorial, service beyond Journal Square to Newark was an extra-fare operation, and as the red MP-38's set out across the Meadows, a conductor would swing through the train collecting tickets.* PATH dropped the extra fare and turned the entire operation into a prepayment system; fences and turnstiles were erected around the New York-bound track at Newark, and a single flat fare takes one from any place in Jersey to any place in New York.

---

* Within the H&M district, conventional subway-style fare collection was employed. On the joint service to Newark, though, railroad-style tickets were used.

Under Port Authority management the route to Newark is no longer the "joint service" of days gone by, but rather a PATH operation exclusively. PATH trains have their own dedicated third-rail trackage that railroad trains may not use or venture upon and which the Port Authority leases from the corporate successors of the PRR for a dollar a year. (One dollar a year to lease the MP-52 cars; a "second dollar" for use of the right of way.) Along the line between Journal Square and Newark, PRR position-light signals soon gave way to mass transit-style color light signals, ac catenary was first deactivated and eventually taken down, and PATH cars used in Newark service no longer had to be equipped with PRR cab signals. Rapid transit-style "trips" placed next to signals at track level now protect against rear-end collisions should a train operator run by a signal into an occupied block. An historical aside: Only PRR-owned cars were fitted with cab signals during "joint service" days; consequently, they had to be positioned on the front and rear of all trains assigned to the Newark route. H&M-owned cars could be coupled only into mid-train positions.

During "joint service" days, H&M actually and literally shared trackage with the railroad beyond Journal Square (*née* Summit Avenue), and motormen were required to pass a **PRR** book-of-rules examination. Since the line could be traveled by either a transit or railroad train, smash-boards were installed at key points to prevent large Pennsy engines from taking incorrectly set turnouts and venturing onto tight trackage reserved for the shorter and narrower H&M equipment.

A further, if minor, modernization is a new code system to identify the various PATH services. In keeping with several other transit systems, PATH has assigned a color code to each route, and has begun the long task of familiarizing the public with the new visual vocabulary. Green identifies New York (*i.e.*, World Trade Center) to Newark trains; red, Hoboken–Thirty-third Street; orange, Hoboken–World Trade Center; blue, Thirty-third Street–Journal Square.

Ridership on the PATH system increased after the Aldene Plan went into effect; in 1971 over 39 million rode the refurbished system. Nevertheless, the parent Port Authority has solid figures to back up its contention that the line will never be a self-sustaining operation. From 1967 to 1968 passenger traffic increased some 14%, but the operating deficit jumped by a devastating 38%. PATH's expenses exceeded income by over $25 million in 1974. The full extent of the fiscal and social dilemma this represents can be seen in the fact that while total ridership on the system today

One of the 1958-built K-class in PATH livery it wore in later years. Car shown, No. 1209, was originally a PRR-owned MP-52 unit.

is about a third of its all-time high, ridership during the peak rush-hour periods is now heavier than it ever was in H&M history. In 1927 peak-hour passenger counts at Hoboken and Newark were 12,400 and 4000 respectively. Today these numbers are 17,000 and 7600. The PATH system is in the curious position of not carrying enough passengers to break even but also not having enough capacity to handle rush-hour crowds.

Deficits or no deficits, PATH has developed an aggressive marketing campaign for its services, and seems bent on reviving the old "Public Be Pleased" spirit of the McAdoo days. Trade publications are always holding the line up as a model for others to emulate, and the system's assortment of booklets, maps and other transit aids are acknowledged to be among the best in the industry.

With the World Trade Center nearing completion, the Port Authority saw the need for additional PATH rolling stock and in late 1970 awarded a contract for sixty-five additional PA-class cars, an order that swelled the company's fleet to just shy of 300 units. An oddity developed when bids were opened; the low bidder was Hawker Siddley Canada Ltd., of Thunder Bay, Ontario, a firm well known for the wartime Hawker Hurricane, and in recent years the supplier of transit equipment for the Toronto subway. Pullman-Standard, the next-lowest bidder, let out an awful howl when PATH entered into contract with the Canadian outfit, and actually petitioned the U.S. Customs Bureau to move against the deal under the statute authority of the 1921 Federal Anti-Dumping Act. But intervention was not forthcoming and in 1972 PATH added yet another "first" to its long list of innovations: "the first non-domestic transit equipment ever to be purchased by a U.S. system."

PATH's Future

The Port of New York Authority—lately renamed the Port Authority of New York and New Jersey—has never been overly aggressive in moving into the rail passenger field. In addition to PATH, for many years its only other passenger rail activity involved leasing fleets of cars to suburban railroads under the provisions of the New York State Commuter Car Program. Indeed, as part of the overall PATH–World Trade Center agreements in 1962, both states passed legislative "covenants" which effectively precluded use of additional Port Authority monies for projects that are not self-sustaining (*e.g.,* mass transit). But political leaders in both states are rapidly developing the conviction that the Authority's extremely strong financial position must be brought to bear on the area's transit difficulties. In 1972, as a result of considerable prodding, the Port Authority announced a $650 million plan to build a rail connection to Kennedy International Airport in New York, a project that took another quarter-century—and many additional millions of dollars—before construction ever got underway.

The early PATH years also saw active discussion of major extensions for the old McAdoo rail transit system, including continuing the Newark line along the PRR main line beyond that city's Penn Station to Elizabeth, where it would bear west along the Jersey Central right-of-way and continue to the suburban community of Plainfield. Also under active consideration was a proposal to have PATH trains serve nearby Newark Airport, either en route to Plainfield or as part of a separate project.

As mass transit policy evolved in northern New Jersey in the final quarter of the twentieth century, improved passenger service to Elizabeth and Plainfield came not from an expansion of the PATH system but by a major upgrade of the area's commuter rail system, developments that will be touched upon in Part Four. But while it has yet to be built—and likely never will be built—a good chunk of this "new extension" of the PATH system has been in daily operation since 1937!

When H&M service began into the new station in Newark, it was planned to continue the transit line beyond the main PRR station at Raymond Boulevard a mile or so to South Street. Here a trolley loop was to be constructed, and certain street cars could connect with the H&M at this point, thus eliminating some congestion downtown. Just about the entire line was built, all except a small bridge over South Street itself. It hasn't been built yet, and the two-track "transit line" that extends west of Newark's Penn Station has been used to store H&M and PATH cars between runs.

The Hudson Tubes (sad to say, PATH's image makers have banished use of the colorful old name) is a proud rail system that is both rich in heritage and full of promise for the future. Old-timers along the Jersey waterfront still pass along stories of the days when the Tubes were being built, and there are yet those who insist

H&M's old Thirty-third Street terminal was demolished during the 1930s to make way for the Sixth Avenue Subway, and the present one built—at Thirty-second Street—after the subway was completed. It was proposed that the City take over the H&M for the new subway's route. This never happened, so here are some PATH spanking-new PA-class cars at "Thirty-third." Compare with bottom illustration on page 22. (Author photo)

bodies of victims from a long-ago construction accident are to this day buried in some sealed-off tunnel beneath the Hudson. But the most macabre legend of all is that of the "headless man." Trackwalkers reputedly refuse to go out on assignments singly for fear of the strange creature who haunts the various tunnels.

Then there's the Thirty-third Street terminal, which by some typically New York strain of logic is actually located at Thirty-second Street.* It is part of an incredible concentration of underground railway activity. If one were to slice through the ground in the Thirty-second–Thirty-third Street area beneath the Avenue of the Americas (Sixth Avenue), the following would be found: four tracks of the Penn Central heading for the East River tunnels and Sunnyside Yards, tracks that also host the LIRR's commuter fleet; four tracks of the BMT Broadway subway; four tracks of the IND Sixth Avenue subway; and finally the three-track terminal where PATH trains load and discharge passengers. And it's all underground and hidden from view.

While it may seem an inappropriate topic to raise, mention must be made of the characteristic *smell* of the H&M system. Not

---

* There's a reasonable explanation for this. The original terminal was at Thirty-third Street, but it was altered when the city built the IND subway in the 1930s. The rebuilt station is a block south of the original, but the older name was retained for convenience's sake.

really offensive and very difficult to describe, the Tubes are possessed of a strong and quite distinctive aroma. The new air-conditioned World Trade Center terminal has banished a good deal of this singularity, but it persists as ever in places like Hoboken, Exchange Place and Grove Street.

The dreams and goals of William McAdoo, then, have a good bit of mileage left in them. And while the idea of an air-conditioned subway train built in Thunder Bay, Ontario, speeding travelers to an airport to catch a Boeing 747 is a little beyond what McAdoo originally had in mind, chances are he'd think it all a fine idea. And so would "Crazy Luke."

Penn Central and Beyond

The New York Tunnel Extension has provided access to and from Manhattan Island for over five million passenger trains since it opened in 1910. True enough, it has waned in proportion to a general decline in rail passenger traffic. But as national policy begins to re-emphasize the value of rail transport, the Hudson River tunnels and the embankment across the Jersey Meadows

Nosing out of tunnel D from Penn Station, a PC GG-1 brings "The Broadway Limited"—its run from Chicago to New York complete—into the daylight en route to Sunnyside Yard. (Author photo)

have again demonstrated the incredible vision of Samuel Rea and George Gibbs.

The Pennsylvania Railroad officially passed from the corporate scene in 1968 through merger with its old rival, the New York Central. In its stead, Penn Central was created and rapidly became living testament to all the ills of the railroad industry. The merger effected considerable alterations in service patterns. So costly was the trans-bay car float operation that ferried freight cars from Greenville to Bay Ridge, for example, that Penn Central eliminated the system, and now routes tonnage from the west and south into New England through Pearlman Yard in Selkirk, N.Y. and across the Hudson by bridge just below Albany.

Passenger service has also been adjusted since the Penn Central merger, but it was the creation of the National Rail Passenger Corporation—Amtrak—in 1971 that has had the more marked influence. Amtrak is a quasi-governmental corporation that assumed operational responsibility for the great bulk of the nation's long distance passenger trains. New York–Washington service has been assigned to a multi-million dollar fleet of sixty-one Budd-built electric multiple-unit cars dubbed the Metroliners. Designed even

A Washington-bound Metroliner zips out of Bergen Portal and into the easy curve atop PRR-built "Chinese wall" embankment. (Author photo)

prior to Amtrak under a Federally-funded research project, these high-speed cars have introduced a truly premium service under the ac catenary. Even as the Metroliners are setting new speed records for domestic passenger trains and eating significantly into the air travel market between New York and Washington, designers are at work on replacement equipment that will allow higher performance levels.

Always a good rail passenger service and a vital component of Amtrak's network is New York–Florida service. PRR was the northern link for trains such as *The East Coast Champion* and *The Silver Meteor,* and Penn Central and Amtrak continue the tradition. Among Amtrak's early actions was the signing of a contract with General Electric for twenty-six 6000 hp electric locomotives to begin replacing the graceful GG-1 on Florida-bound schedules, as well as other assignments under the wires. The new C+C locomotives are known as the E60CP units and the first engine—No. 951—was completed in the final weeks of 1974.

Other changes: Amtrak and Penn Central have routed all New England service into Penn Station via the Hell Gate Bridge and East River tunnels, eschewing Grand Central. The ac electrification on the Pennsylvania and on the New Haven railroads was compatible, and GG-1's, Metroliners, and now the new GE motors operate over both systems with no regard for the corporate demarcation which New York once represented on through schedules. Yet another novelty in Amtrak's New England service is something called the "Turbotrain," a jet-powered articulated trainset built by United Aircraft for operation between New York and Boston. Its speed capabilities are severely restricted by the present condition of the ex-New Haven roadbed, but it is an interesting contemporary addition to operations in the New York area, and may well presage the future style of inter-city passenger trains. In 1974 Amtrak ordered seven more turbine trains of a slightly different sort for the New York–Boston market.*

In addition to long-haul service, commuters are a serious force to be dealt with in today's rail passenger picture. Pennsy's one-time stepchild, the Long Island, has gone through an interesting evolution since it operated the first train into Penn Station in 1910. Following World War II, LIRR left the Pennsy "family" and became, essentially, an independent railroad. PRR remained

---

* While powered normally by jet engines, the Turbotrain also is equipped with electric motors and third rail shoes for operation through the tunnels into Penn Station.

MP-54s and (in background) a LIRR double-decker in a scene characteristic of heavy density suburban railroading—electric trains and advertising on every available surface! Date this one 1969. (Author photo)

a major LIRR creditor, however, despite the fact that tuscan red was ruled taboo on cars and stations. Even with exceptional tax relief, and no hounding from the Pennsylvania for its deferred obligations, the financial problems of commuter service eventually proved impossible to solve within the context of private enterprise. In 1965 the Long Island Rail Road became a publicly owned and operated endeavor, and is today a component of the Metropolitan Transportation Authority of New York State. Operations continue into Penn Station through the East River Tunnels, but MTA also built in a new tunnel that will eventually bring LIRR trains into Manhattan at Sixty-third Street, where they will be routed into Grand Central. The new bore is a four-track, two-level structure that will be shared by LIRR and subway trains.

On a hot and hazy summer afternoon in 1955, a pair of GG-1's have moved out of Sunnyside Yard in Long Island City and are waiting for signal authorization to proceed into the East River tunnels and board passengers at Penn Station.

Commuter service on the former PRR lines west out of New York have benefited from financial assistance from the State of New Jersey. GG-1's and aging MP-54 multiple-unit cars were replaced by sleek stainless steel electric cars called the "Jersey Arrows." Planning agencies in the New York–New Jersey area began to discuss such proposals as funneling suburban service operated by the Erie–Lackawanna Railroad into Manhattan through the 1910-built Hudson River tunnels, and even constructing a brand new set of tubes to handle the increased commuter rail service they envision as inevitable.

The cycles have been interesting, and the future now appears bright. Turbotrains and Metroliners, northeast corridor and Amtrak, World Trade Center and PATH, Jersey DOT and MTA—the names have changed but underlying it all remains the solid achievements that were realized in the early years of the twentieth century by the Pennsylvania Railroad—and McAdoo's H&M.

Train No. 174, "The Colonial," emerges from the Hudson River tunnels and twists through the slip switches in the small out-of-doors area just before entering Penn Station. (Author photo)

The Seventh Avenue façade of Penn Station looking uptown from West 31st Street. (Library of Congress)

Epilogue: AN ODE TO PENN STATION

ASK ANY Manhattan taxi driver to take you to "Thirty-third and Seventh" and he'll likely respond: "Oh yeah, Penn Station." But the fact is that while New Yorkers continue to use an older nomenclature, Penn Station is—well, it's gone. In an act which *The New York Times* decried as "monumental vandalism," and which drew sustained criticism the world over, the wonderful, beautiful, classic station was torn down in 1965 and replaced by a twenty-nine-story office building and a 19,000-seat sports arena that bears the traditional New York name of Madison Square Garden. With fitting irony the project carried a price tag of $116 million—the exact cost of the entire New York Tunnel Extension in 1910.

Because tracks and platforms at Penn Station are and were located below ground level, trains, thankfully, are still running and the developer, in cooperation with the railroad, was able to build a new station in the basement of his project. It was not an easy trick to pull off. Something like five hundred new support columns were drilled to bedrock around and between departing trains, and amid it all railroad passengers had to be routed to appropriate platforms "through corridors of plywood and saw horses in a sort of mouse-in-a-maze game," as *Business Week* noted. But the original terminal building—the seemingly ageless capstone of the New York Tunnel Extension—is no more.

It would be pointless to rehash the arguments that were, *and are still,* put forth both for and against the new Penn Station project. It is equally inappropriate to judge the aesthetics of the "new Penn Station" by the old. In point of fact the new terminal is attractive, functional, even pleasant, its only shortcomings developing from inevitable contrasts with its stately predecessor. Suffice it to say it was critical for New York to improve its tax base and general business climate by constructing new office space, and the good sense of locating a major sports complex near public transportation is self-evident. But despite it all, and even in the face of the fact that the loss of Penn Station was instrumental in calling national attention to the folly of destroying old and cherished landmarks, there are those whose bitterness will never be assuaged, and who regard the demise of Penn Station as a total and unredeemable catastrophe.

To conclude our treatment of rails under the Hudson River, let us pay homage to that fine old station. Not in bitter remorse over the fact it is no longer in existence; rather in rightful celebration of its grandeur and majesty.

It has often been said that Penn Station was a "replica" of the baths of Caracalla in Rome. This is not quite true; in fact it was modeled after a variety of classic structures. *Scientific American,* for example, noted in 1910 that "while fully adapted to modern ideas," the station was "suggested by the great halls and basilicas of Rome, such as the baths of Caracalla, Titus and Diocletian, and the basilica of Constantine."

But mere modeling of ancient architecture was not the goal of Penn Station's designers. The building was fully functional, and futhermore, its larger and more imposing themes were developed to suggest the gateway character that the terminal in fact fulfilled for so many years. Some said the Seventh Avenue facade resembled the Brandenburg Gate in Berlin; another commentator felt that "beneath all the suggestions of Roman temples and baths is a clear impression that here is one of the leading railway stations in the world."

The site of Penn Station and its approaches required the excavation of three million cubic yards, and the cavernous maw this created in midtown Manhattan was frequently likened to the then a-building Panama Canal. The terminal itself was located between Seventh and Eighth Avenues, and Thirty-first and Thirty-third Streets; to the west, between Eighth and Ninth avenues and the same side streets, a large Post Office was constructed—designed

The ticket concourse. (Library of Congress)

by the architect of Penn Station and with chutes, ramps and conveyor belts leading directly to trackside. Modest storage yards were located in an open cut between Ninth and Tenth Avenues.

The station building measured 784 by 430 feet, and at its maximum was 153 feet high. The first stone work was installed on June 15, 1908, and the masons had completed their tasks thirteen months later. The building's outside walls required

490,000 cubic feet of "pink granite"; this and 60,000 cubic feet of interior stone was transported to the site in 1140 freight cars from quarries in Milford, Massachusetts. Total tonnage was 47,000.

To continue a bit with overwhelming numbers: Penn Station required 26,000 tons of steel and 15,000 individual bricks. When it was completed illumination was supplied by 30,000 electric light bulbs. Indeed no aspect of the terminal was beyond public interest. It was reported, for instance, in very serious language that a "Mr. Michael J. McAloon, of Boston" was selected from several contenders and awarded the "shoe blackening privilege."

On the operational side, the terminal was outfitted with 231 color light signals, 45 double-slip switches with movable point frogs, one single-slip switch, and 90 conventional switches. All this complexity was governed by four switch towers—named, rather prosaically, Towers A, B, C and D. Of these, Tower A, controlling the western approach, is the key nerve center. For most of its life, Tower A was—and remains today—sequestered in the "basement," so to speak, of the General Post Office. When Penn Station opened, though, and before the Post Office was built, Tower A was a free-standing structure located in broad daylight between Eighth and Ninth Avenues and stradling tracks 10 through 13. It was topped off with a grand mission-style tile roof.

More operational details: all twenty-one terminal tracks led into the Hudson River tunnels. This was not the case, however on the East River end. Tracks 1 through 4 stub-end at Seventh Avenue and provide no access at all to the East River tunnels.* Tunnels A and B under Thirty-third Street—the tubes used principally by LIRR trains—feed into tracks 14 through 21. Tunnels C and D under Thirty-second Street—used principally by PRR and later New Haven trains—feed into tracks 5 through 17.

The Seventh Avenue side of the building featured a most impressive Roman Doric colonnade, and it was this which suggested Brandenburg. Stone columns four feet six inches in diameter, and thirty-five feet high, were set off by a massive clock in the center.

With Charles Follen McKim in charge, the firm of McKim, Mead and White designed Penn Station. Surely the terminal's most impressive component was the great train concourse. It was from here that passengers descended to trackside, and the 340-by-210-foot room—perhaps "courtyard" is a more appropriate term

---

* When Penn Station was designed, planners envisioned a fifth and sixth East River tunnel that would have fed into this part of the terminal.

A 1910 trackside view in Penn Station just before service was inaugurated. (Library of Congress)

—was topped off with a dazzling blend of glass domes, panels, and arches, all supported by graceful lattice steel girders. Rarely has there ever been an interior space whose mood could change so totally as bright morning sunlight faded into late afternoon, and then again as daylight itself gave way to the infinite black of night. The glass ceiling would cascade sunlight down onto endless throngs of daytime passengers heading for South Amboy or Saint Louis, and the same ceiling would give the concourse a completely different appearance in the after-midnight hours, as crews of porters went about their tasks and a few straggling passengers waited for a 3:00 A.M. train for Baltimore, with only the station's lights providing illumination under the now-dark glass-work.

The architectural drama of the train concourse was heightened by the station's layout, which led passengers into the vastness of the skylighted area. In his book *Lost New York,* author Nathan Silver claims that Penn Station was a magnificent blend of classic and machine cultures—the stone masonry of the station's exterior leading into the Crystal Palace motif of the concourse.

Of course, while it was the sweep of the station's architecture, and the impact of the concourse that were its dominant themes, personal memories of Penn Station often fix on lesser features: the wrought iron gates and railings and always-polished brass handrails—the haze that seemed to settle over the concourse as afternoon sunlight flooded in from the west—the infinite variety of timetables from all over North America regularly stocked by the information counter in the days when double-roomettes and reserved coach seats were the principal means of inter-city travel—the total incongruity of Lehigh Valley passenger trains arriving and departing on their daily schedules.*

Over the years Penn Station maintained a style and grace that was unusual for a public building. The concourse became, surely, the "best known room" in all America, and through its gates passed millions upon millions of passengers heading off to a Florida vacation, four years at college, the bedside of a dying parent. Nor was the station a stranger to the high and mighty. In the years before anyone ever heard of "Air Force One," the nation's chief executive would regularly arrive in New York aboard a POTUS special (*i.e.,* President Of The United States). Such trains would leave and depart from tracks 11 and 12 because these lead directly into the Hudson River tunnels and required no lateral switching.

Perhaps it was Thomas Wolfe who best expressed the true *élan* of Penn Station. In *You Can't Go Home Again* he contends that the station actually captured time itself within its walls and vaults. But this was published in 1940. Penn Station would throb as never before under the press of wartime traffic, but following VJ Day the nation's travel habits began to change. No longer would the "Broadway" go out in several sections and gone were the days when the terminal was a main gateway to the heartland of America.

In its final years the waiting room suffered a tasteless indignity when a futuristic-looking counter was installed smack in the middle of the floor, and the stately old ticket windows were abandoned. Additionally, lighted advertisements were hung from the walls, creating an appearance that Lewis Mumford described as "a vast jukebox." But these affronts can today be regarded as minor. The ultimate catastrophe was to take place in 1965.

The original Penn Station was a New York fixture for fifty-five years, from 1910 through 1965. Then, as the twentieth century was

---

* During World War I, when all U.S. railroads were placed under governmental control—with one W. G. McAdoo as the man in charge—the Pennsylvania was forced to share its Manhattan terminal with both the Lehigh Valley and the Baltimore and Ohio. Both roads' passenger trains were hauled under the Hudson by DD-1's. B&O resumed its former ways after the war, but Lehigh Valley continued as a tenant until the line abandoned passenger service in 1961.

The train concourse. (Library of Congress)

nearing its appointed end, low and behold it began to appear that it just might be possible to recapture and recreate some of the glories wrought by McKim, Mead and White almost a century earlier.

Recall that the same architects who created Penn Station also designed a marvelous post office building directly across Eighth Avenue from the famous terminal, and recall, too, that the post office straddles the western end of most of Penn Station's platforms. What appears to be on the verge of happening (at this writing in 2001 a few details remain to be worked out) is that a sizable portion of the central court in the post office building, now named in honor of Franklin D. Roosevelt's legendary postmaster general, James A. Farley, will be converted into ticket offices and other facilities for Amtrak's intercity passengers; direct access will be established between this concourse and the platforms where passengers board Amtrak trains. While New Jersey Transit and Long Island commuters will continue to be accommodated in the current facility under Madison Square Garden, "Penn Station" may well rise again!

Will the advent of such a project assuage the loss of the original Penn Station? Clearly the answer to this question must be "no." But when fortune and circumstance combine to make a McKim, Mead and White-designed building across the street from Penn Station available for railroad purposes, it must certainly be regarded as an eminently positive development.

Part Four: INTO A NEW CENTURY
(Developments under the mighty Hudson
since the first edition)

DURING THE FINAL QUARTER of the twentieth century, PATH exhibited remarkable steadiness and stability. Railroad service across the New York Tunnel Extension and under the Hudson River into Penn Station, on the other hand, saw substantial transformation and change.

PATH

Under Port Authority auspices, PATH continued to upgrade and modernize the aging H&M plant. Stations were rehabilitated, a new state-of-the-art control center named in honor of veteran PATH executive John Hoban was opened at Journal Square, the system's older maintenance shop in Jersey City was replaced with a modern-as-tomorrow facility in Harrison, New Jersey, adjacent to the site of Manhattan Transfer, and the K-class cars of 1958 were retired when additional PA-class equipment was added to the roster in the late 1980s.

The PA-4 units, as the newest cars are called, differ slightly from earlier PA equipment. Instead of two sets of twin doors per side per car, the PA-4's have three, to speed passenger boarding. Because these units are unpainted brushed aluminum, PATH repainted earlier PA equipment in more neutral tones to complement this new hue. Body shells for the PA-4 units were constructed in Japan by Kawasaki, with final assembly taking place in Yonkers, New York. Earlier PA units were rebuilt to ensure dependable operation as well as compatibility with the newer cars.

Before rebuilding older PA rolling stock, PATH undertook a

A train of PA-4 units is about to depart Journal Square for 33rd Street in midtown Manhattan. A major difference between PA-4 equipment and earlier PA cars is the inclusion of three sets of doors along each side of the newer equipment.

It is late afternoon, the sun is setting, evening commuters are heading home, and a PATH train from New York approaches Journal Square.

rigorous analysis to determine if it would be more cost effective to replace this equipment with new cars. The study concluded that rehabilitation was a smarter course of action that would extend the useful life of the cars by a number of years, although it is likely that PA-1, PA-2, and PA-3 units will be replaced with new equipment early in the twenty-first century.

What did not happen to PATH, though, was any kind of route expansion. Talk of extending the old line out to Plainfield never advanced beyond the planning stage and it now appears that the original H&M limits of 1911—with Penn Station, Newark, of course, replacing the line's original terminal at Park Place—will continue to define the PATH system for the foreseeable future.

Instead, what expanded rail mass transportation the northern New Jersey area required—and there was quite a bit of it—primarily involved upgrading and improving the area's commuter rail services. In addition, the first elements of a new light rail transit line that will eventually encompass twenty miles opened for business along the Hudson River waterfront in April 2000, linking Bayonne and Jersey City. Eventually, the new line will reach Hoboken, Weehawkeen, and Secaucus, paralleling PATH between Exchange Place and Hoboken.

All of this new transit investment has underscored the important role PATH plays, since the one-time McAdoo tunnels remain an important link for commuters en route to jobs in Manhattan, and they provide the only direct rail service between New Jersey and the financial district of lower Manhattan. In a development that can only be called ironic, because the PATH system operates at virtual capacity during peak rush hours, in the late 1980s the Port Authority revived an old transport concept to provide additional trans-Hudson passenger capacity: ferryboats.

Privately-operated by New York Waterway under contract to the Port Authority, the new vessels link the World Trade Center with landings on the New Jersey side, including the old Lackawanna Terminal in Hoboken, the only remaining passenger terminal on the west bank of the Hudson River still in operation as such and a location where PATH boards large numbers of New York-bound passengers each day. WTC–Hoboken ferry service was formally inaugurated on October 11, 1989, and within a decade patronage had grown to two-and-a-half million trips a year. While this is less than four percent of the passengers who ride PATH, it represents an expansion of trans-Hudson capacity by that amount or more, and since PATH continues to operate at capacity during peak hours, the new ferries are a useful way to provide new options for Manhattan-bound commuters.

(NY Waterway, incidentally, is a rather important success story in New York Harbor, operating a variety of new ferry crossings in addition to Port Authority-sponsored routes, as well as sightseeing services and special shuttles, in season, to the area's two major-league baseball parks, Shea Stadium and Yankee Stadium.)

The following table displays a variety of recent statistical information describing the one-time McAdoo Tubes as they begin a new century of service.

PATH Profile
Data reflect FY 1998

No. passenger cars available	347
No. passenger cars required to meet peak-hour assignments	267
Annual passenger trips	69.9 million
Average passengers per weekday	237,310
Length of route: one way	13.8 miles
Length of route: one way (in tunnel)	7.4 miles
Total trackage	43.1 miles
Annual operating expenses	$147 million
Expenses realized through passenger fares	33%

AMTRAK

In the final quarter of the twentieth century, Amtrak matured into a steady and permanent presence on the New York rail scene, a worthy and appropriate successor to the Pennsylvania Railroad. True, fiscal and political problems have managed to keep the agency in a state of semi-permanent crisis since its founding in 1971, but in terms of the service it provides, at the end of an old century and the beginning of a new, Amtrak could boast an impressive list of accomplishments.

One measure of how Amtrak has transformed service under the Hudson River into and out of New York's Penn Station can be seen in the agency's experiences in the area of motive power for its passenger trains, an evolution that began when PRR put the first DD-1 in service in 1910.

Amtrak's first effort to design and build a new high-speed electric locomotive was not an outstanding success. The first of twenty-six locomotives that were designated the E60 class arrived on the property from the Erie, Pennsylvania, works of General Electric in

Amtrak's GE-built E60 electric locomotives were not successful as high-speed motive power along the Northeast Corridor, but served well on the electrified portion of long-distance trains, such as Florida-New York No. 82, "The Silver Star," here heading north through Maryland countryside outside Washington, DC.

October of 1974. Unfortunately, the new heavyweight units did not track well at speeds in excess of 100 m.p.h. and as a result they spent the majority of their time working such schedules as Amtrak's New York–Philadelphia service, as well as the NEC portion of trains originating in New York and bound for such far-away points as Miami, New Orleans, and Chicago. While these are important passenger services, they do not require the kind of high-speed operation that Amtrak was determined to make the hallmark of its service between points along the Northeast Corridor itself.

Rather than designing another new electric locomotive from the ground up, Amtrak decided that a better course of action would be to import several state-of-the-art electric locomotives from Europe and to test them in Northeast Corridor service. Two popular European designs were so selected.

The first, built in Sweden by ASEA and designated the Rc4a there, was a mainstay along the electrified main lines of SJC, the Swedish state railway. A production model was modified to meet North American service and regulatory requirements and shipped to the United States in July 1976. Identified as No. X995 during its time with Amtrak, the Swedish locomotive was tested and then put into revenue service. The second candidate locomotive was built in France by Alsthom and was a design then popular on SNCF, the French national railway. It was delivered to the port of Baltimore in January 1977 and assigned the number X996 by Amtrak. Because of trackage and catenary incompatibilities, though, the testing of the X996 never advanced to the point where the locomotive entered revenue service.

Meanwhile, the ASEA design had performed quite well, and over the winter of 1977–78 Amtrak ordered the initial production models of a fleet that would eventually total 53 units. Amtrak contracted with the Electro-Motive Division (EMD) of General Motors for these new locomotives, as EMD was the North American licensee for ASEA. ASEA produced the internal electrical equipment for the locomotives, while EMD subcontracted the construction of their car bodies to the Budd Company of Philadelphia. New AEM-7 class locomotives, as they were designated, moved down the Budd assembly line in tandem with new Amfleet passengers cars they would soon haul up and down the Northeast Corridor. When the testing program was over, both the X995 and the X996 were returned to Europe where they joined the fleets of SJC and SNCF, respectively.

The AEM-7 quickly became a fixture along Amtrak's Northeast Corridor, allowing the legendary GG-1 to be retired, displacing the original electric multiple-unit cars in Metroliner service, and earning an excellent reputation for performance and dependability. The authoritative *Car and Locomotive Cyclopedia* was so impressed with the AEM-7 that it remarked; "Not since the introduction of New York Central's J-class Hudson steam locomotive in 1927 has a new locomotive model had such impact on speeds and schedule upgrades."

In addition to Amtrak, three different regional mass transit agencies that evolved to assume responsibility for commuter service on electrified segments of the Pennsylvania Railroad within their respective territories also adopted the basic ASEA design. MARC, an agency of the state of Maryland, acquired four AEM-7's for service out of Baltimore and Washington, while SEPTA, the transit agency in Philadelphia, purchased eight units. New Jersey Transit, a public agency responsible for commuter service into and out of Penn Station and about which more will be said presently, contracted for 32 units of a slightly different version of the ASEA design. (To be precise, seven of the SEPTA units are true AEM-7's,

The AEM-7 electric was based on a Swedish design that Amtrak tested before ordering production-model locomotives. No. 906 is rolling into Newark with a Washington–New York Metroliner schedule in 2000. Success of these electric locomotives allowed Amtrak to phase out the multiple-unit cars that inaugurated Metroliner service.

while one is akin to the NJ Transit variation on the basic ASEA design.)

Amtrak trains hauled by new AEM-7's became the rule between New Haven, New York, and Washington in the final quarter of the twentieth century. Indeed, it was behind a pair of AEM-7 locomotives—Nos. 937 and 933—that that the first revenue train inaugurated electrified service into Boston on January 28, 2000, as Amtrak realized a long-held corporate goal of turning the entire Boston–Washington Northeast Corridor into a fully electrified railroad.

The advent of electrification along the Shore Line of the former New York, New Haven and Hartford Railroad between New Haven and Boston also saw Amtrak design a new generation of electric-powered equipment for NEC service. By this time, high-speed passenger service in countries throughout the world had shifted to a different concept than locomotives hauling trains of separate cars. New, state-of-the-art equipment consisted in trainsets, so called—fixed consists with "power cars" at either one or both ends, and an ability to operate equally well in either direction. Power cars are essentially locomotives, but they share the look and the line of the

Amtrak's standard rolling stock on Northeast Corridor trains during the last quarter of the twentieth century was a fleet of Budd-built stainless steel cars popularly known as the Amfleet.

rolling stock they haul and are generally not able to be used for any locomotive-like purposes other than powering fixed-consist trainsets. Given the three-digit speed such equipment routinely maintains, the forward end of a power car is severely streamlined. Trainsets that are powered by a single power car typically have an equally streamlined control station at the opposite end to permit operation in either direction. Trains such as the famous Shinkansen in Japan and the TGV in France all utilize such equipment.

Harking back to its testing of two European locomotives before settling on the AEM-7 design in the mid-1970s, Amtrak imported two contemporary trainsets from Europe in the early 1990s for evaluation. One came from Germany and was known by the acronym ICE, for Inter-City Express. The other trainset was called the X-2000 and was an example of the latest in high-speed rail passenger technology from Sweden.

This time, though, it was less a matter of choosing one trainset or the other as much as it involved developing a unique set of Amtrak specifications based on desirable features from either, or both, of the two test trains. What thus emerged was a trainset featuring six passenger cars flanked by twin power cars and including a "tilting" feature that enables the newcomers to negotiate curves at speed. (Passenger-carrying cars "tilt," power cars do not.) A joint venture of the Canadian rail car manufacturer Bombardier and the French transportation consortium called Alstom was awarded a contract to construct twenty such trainsets. (For whatever reason, the spelling of the French consortium's name has mutated from "Alsthom" to "Alstom.") The first trainset built to Amtrak's new specifications entered revenue service in December 2000.

The new trainsets are designed to operate comfortably at speeds up to 150 m.p.h., a substantial advance beyond the 120 m.p.h. that represents the practical upper-limit of AEM-7-powered trains. Of course there are few locations along the Northeast Corridor where such speeds will be possible; thus, the new equipment will reduce terminal-to-terminal running times not so much by their top speed as by their ability to take curves faster.

While engineering and manufacturing work was moving forward on the new trains, Amtrak's marketing people decided that a new service name was needed to signal the onset of the new equipment and the new service it would provide. Thus was born Acela, successor to a variety of nomenclature that had evolved around Amtrak's Northeast Corridor product but that lacked the kind of sharply focused consumer identity the railroad felt was necessary. The popular Metroliner designation, once the hallmark of Amtrak's high-speed efforts between Washington and New York, thus joins traditional PRR nomenclature like *The Morning Congressional* as no longer descriptive of rail service in and out of Penn Station. The new high-speed trainsets will provide premium-fare Acela Express service, while other Northeast Corridor operations will be identified as Acela Regional and Acela Commuter.

In addition to the twenty new Acela trainsets, Amtrak also placed an order with Bombardier-Alstom for a new class of electric locomotives known as the HHP-8; the initial order was for fifteen units. Externally, these new 8,000 h.p. locomotives bear a strong resemblance to Acela power cars, the major visual difference being that they have cabs at both ends and will function as true locomotives. Like Acela trainsets, the HHP-8's have a top speed of 150 m.p.h. They will supplement the AEM-7 fleet and allow the last of Amtrak's E60-class locomotives to be retired.

Finally, with respect to Amtrak developments in the final years of the twentieth century, a major project that was completed in 1991 allowed the carrier to consolidate all of its New York operations at Penn Station.

An Acela Express, led by power car No. 2039, has arrived in Washington after a fast run from New York's Penn Station.

Amtrak's HHP-8 electric locomotives have a look that is similar to power cars on Acela Express trainsets.

Previously, Amtrak's Empire Corridor trains that operated up the Hudson River to Albany, Buffalo, and points north and west over the former New York Central Railroad were boarded at Grand Central Terminal on the east side of Manhattan. Because there was a little-used freight railroad along the west side of Manhattan—it was originally the Hudson River Railroad's entry into New York—Amtrak was able to upgrade this line and bring its trains down the west side, where entry into Penn Station was achieved by punching a hole in a concrete retaining wall at Tenth Avenue. Now passengers can negotiate their way from, say, Baltimore to Syracuse without the thrill of a midtown Manhattan taxi ride. (Grand Central remains a very busy rail terminal, but it no longer dispatches any long-distance trains, only commuter services into suburbs north and northeast of New York.) The locomotives Amtrak uses for Empire Service into Penn Station are otherwise conventional diesel-electric engines that are able to draw dc current from Penn Station's trackside third rail, supplemented by turbine-powered trainsets which Amtrak acquired in the late 1970s but which never quite lived up to initial expectations; these are also equipped with auxiliary electric motors for terminal operations. As part of Amtrak's make-over of the Northeast Corridor under the new Acela name, Empire Service will become part of the Acela Regional designation.

The last quarter of the twentieth century actually saw *two* holes punched in the Tenth Avenue retaining wall. The other gives LIRR trains access to a new storage yard to the west of Penn Station which allows out-of-service trains to remain in Manhattan between morning and evening rush hours, thus eliminating an expensive and inefficient pattern of deadheading trains between Penn Station and storage yards on Long Island at the end of the morning rush and prior to the evening one, as was previously the rule. Amtrak and the LIRR have also designed a new unified control center to oversee Penn Station operations, replacing four older towers that dated back to the terminal's opening in 1910.

New Jersey Transit

As mentioned earlier in Part Three, the state of New Jersey began to provide assistance to commuter passenger railroads operating in the bedroom suburbs of the state's northern counties in the late 1960s. Public assistance helped railroads like the Erie Lackawanna, the Jersey Central, and the Penn Central acquire new rolling stock, but in retrospect, the efforts would have to be described as more *ad hoc* than part of any long-range strategic transportation plan.

The railroads themselves, of course, were hardly in robust condition. Indeed, so poor was their outlook and so bleak seemed their future that in the mid-1970s the federal government established the Consolidated Rail Corporation—Conrail—an amalgamation of seven failing northeast railroads, Penn Central by far the largest, that took over on April 1, 1976.

The legislative purpose behind the creation of Conrail was not to establish another entity requiring massive governmental subsidies on a steady basis. From the outset Conrail was seen as something that must eventually stand on its own in the private sector. And, indeed, so it would.*

To help focus Conrail's attention on its core business of freight transportation, Congress mandated that any and all commuter operations on the Conrail system must either be handed over to regional mass transit agencies, or else be eliminated outright. The statutory deadline for such change was set as January 1, 1983, and it was within such a context that commuter rail services previously operated by a number of different Conrail predecessor railroads were unified under the aegis of a public agency known as New Jersey Transit (NJT).

Initially, NJT's goal was simply the preservation of a variety of commuter services that still reflected the corporate cultures of their diverse origins. Slowly, though, NJT was able to shift its focus from preservation to consolidation, and finally from consolidation to expansion. Central to all the agency's plans in northern New Jersey was the desire to make maximum possible use of the New York Tunnel Extension and the Hudson River tunnels into New York.

One of the pre-Conrail components of NJT was a 67-mile electrified network of suburban routes known as the Morris and Essex Lines, once part of the Delaware, Lackawanna and Western Railroad. They terminated on the banks of the Hudson River at the Lackawanna's Hoboken Terminal and utilized a unique 3,000-volt dc electrification system distributed by overhead catenary. It was a system that lacked any compatibility with the ac system the Pennsylvania had installed along its lines.

---

* Conrail's success is best measured by the fact that in the late 1990s it was sold to two sound and profitable eastern railroads. CSX Corporation acquired, essentially, those elements of Conrail that were originally the New York Central, while Norfolk and Western took title to Conrail lines that once constituted the Pennsylvania Railroad. Conrail's ultimate achievement, in one sense, could be said that it managed to undo the Penn Central merger of 1968. CSX and NS took over their respective elements of Conrail on June 1, 1999.

Because the electrification system on the Morris and Essex Lines was in need of extensive rehabilitation, it was wisely decided that any capital investment should not merely restore the system to its original condition, but render it compatible with the ac system on the one-time PRR as well. DL&W electric lines run parallel to the Pennsy main line adjacent to the site of Manhattan Transfer, and after the dc system was upgraded and converted to ac in 1984, a junction between the two lines was designed and constructed. Since 1996, NJ Transit trains from suburban locations such as Dover and Short Hills have operated into Manhattan through Alexander Cassatt's Hudson River tunnels. NJT coined the service name Midtown Direct for this new operation into Penn Station. While the junction was under construction, the $61 million project was known as the Kearny Connection.*

Even before Midtown Direct was in service, work began on a larger project called Secaucus Transfer. This involves the construction of a station along the New York Tunnel Extension in the middle of the Jersey Meadows where passengers will transfer between commuter trains heading into and out of Penn Station and NJT trains operating over two different lines that were once part of the Erie Railroad and that terminate at the one-time DL&W Terminal in Hoboken.

While this may sound like a rather modest project—it does not involve routing trains into different terminals, as did Midtown Direct—it is anything but modest, as its $450 million cost clearly suggests. The new station itself is along the alignment of the original New York Tunnel Extension, while new "outside" tracks have been built so that Amtrak's high-speed Northeast Corridor trains will not be slowed or delayed by trains stopping at the transfer facility. Upgraded signals and the last word in computer-assisted dispatching systems will ensure that the twin Hudson River tunnels that have been in continuous service since 1910 will be able to handle an expanded volume of service. (See Appendix D.).

With respect to commuter rolling stock, New Jersey initially felt that electric multiple unit cars would be the agency's basic equipment for service on electrified lines and the Jersey Arrow cars that began to replace PRR's MP-54's back in the late 1960s—later

---

* Electrification along Amtrak's Northeast Corridor continues to use an 11,000-volt ac system, while the rehabilitated DL&W electrification is 25,000 volts. (Amtrak's extension of electrified service from New Haven to Boston utilizes a similar 25,000-volt system.) Modern ac electrified equipment operates equally well from either voltage, although engineers of trains moving from one system to the other have to be mindful to "flip a switch" in the cab as they make the transition.

A three-car train of New Jersey Transit Arrow I electric multiple-unit cars heads across the New York Tunnel Extension toward the Hudson River tunnels and Penn Station in 1974. These cars have since been converted into locomotive-hauled coaches.

designated the Arrow I fleet—were expanded as Arrow II and Arrow III cars were delivered in the 1970s. More recently, though, NJ Transit has been moving in a different direction. Its newest equipment for service in electrified territory involves conventional suburban passenger coaches hauled by new electric locomotives. NJT initially opted for a locomotive that was derived from Amtrak's AEM-7 design and thirty-two ALP-class locomotives, as they are designated, were acquired; the first such unit, bearing the number 4400, entered service in early 1990. These locomotives will be supplemented early in the twenty-first century by at least two dozen units that are based on a new German design and are also similar to Amtrak's latest HHP-8 units. Each of these new locomotives carries a price tag in excess of $6 million. (Before buying new electric locomotives of its own, NJT took title to a number of ex-PRR GG-1's, as well as several Amtrak E60's. Indeed, it was NJT, and not Amtrak, that operated the final GG-1 in revenue passenger service, a benchmark that was achieved on October 28, 1983.)

Why electric locomotives have replaced multiple-unit cars as NJ Transit's motive power of choice involves a number of factors.

Cars like No. 1324, a member of NJ Transit's Arrow III fleet, were the only electric multiple-unit cars regularly operating into and out of Penn Station in the early years of the twenty-first century.

Passenger cars are indifferent as to whether they are hauled by diesel or electric locomotives. NJT can thus acquire new rolling stock and assign it indiscriminately to its electrified service or its diesel-powered routes. In addition, contemporary commuter rolling stock is generally rigged for something called "push-pull" operation. What this means is that while the locomotive remains firmly coupled to one end of the train, its engineer can operate the train either from the locomotive ("pull") or from a small cab located in the end vestibule of a passenger car on the opposite end of the train ("push"). Such a train thus enjoys all the bi-directional flexibility once thought to be the province of multiple-unit cars alone. Indeed, NJT has actually converted some of its earlier Arrow I electric multiple-unit cars into unpowered trailer units for use behind its new electric locomotives. Following such conversion, cars also change names—"Arrows" become "Comets."

New Jersey Transit may yet order new electric multiple-unit cars. Pending any such acquisition, though, there was but a single class of electric m.u. equipment operating across the New York Tunnel Extension and into Penn Station in the early years of the new century. This was a fleet of 230 cars built by AVCO/General Electric in 1977–78—and substantially rebuilt with more modern electrical components in the mid-1990s—and known as the Arrow III units. The last of the Arrow II cars, built in 1974–75, were retired from service in early 1998.

In addition to rendering the electrification system on the one-time DL&W lines compatible with that on the Pennsy, NJT also expanded the reach of its electrified services into territory previously served only by diesel-powered trains. Relatively minor extensions have been added to the DL&W's Morris and Essex Lines, while wires have been extended southward from South Amboy to Long Branch along a very important and popular commuter line that parallels the Jersey coast and was once known as the New York and Long Branch Railroad. Long before NJ Transit came on the scene, passenger service on the NY&LB was jointly operated by the Pennsylvania and the Jersey Central.

The story of rails under the mighty Hudson River has not ended, of course, and likely never will. It continues day in and day out and constitutes a vital element in the transportation infrastructure of New York.

A train of "McAdoo reds" heads toward the Hackensack River bridge en route to Hudson Terminal in 1949. The author took this photo with a Brownie camera on his very first trip over "joint service" trackage.

BIBLIOGRAPHY
(Suggested Further Reading)

Baehr, Guy T. "Conrail Bows Out of Urban Transit," *Mass Transit* 10 (January 1983), 50–53.

———, "Keeping the (Political) Faith and PATH's 30 cent Fare," *Mass Transit* 10 (October 1982), 64–66, 70.

Bezilla, Michael. "The Pennsylvania's P5/P5a Electric Locomotives," *The Keystone* 12 (March 1979), 4–15.

Burgess, George H. and Miles C. Kennedy. *Centennial History of the Pennsylvania Railroad Company* (Philadelphia: The Pennsylvania Railroad, 1949).

Burr, S. D. V. *Tunneling Under the Hudson River* (New York: John Wiley and Sons, 1985).

Carleton, Paul. *The Hudson & Manhattan Railroad Revisited* (Dunnellon, FL: D. Carleton Railbooks, 1990).

Couper, William (ed.). *History of the Engineering Construction and Equipment of the Pennsylvania Railroad Company's New York Terminal and Approaches* (New York: Blanchard, 1912).

Cudahy, Brian J. *Over and Back; the History of Ferryboats in New York Harbor* (New York: Fordham University Press, 1990).

Diehl, Lorraine B. *The Late, Great Pennsylvania Station* (New York: American Heritage, 1985).

Dos Passos, John. *Manhattan Transfer* (Boston: Houghton Mifflin, 1925).

Dreiser, Theodore. *Best Short Stories of Theodore Dreiser* (New York: World, 1927).

Droege, John A. *Passenger Terminals and Trains* (New York: McGraw Hill, 1916; Milwaukee: Kalmbach, 1969).

Fitzherbert, Anthony. *"The Public Be Pleased": William G. McAdoo and the Hudson Tubes* (New York: Electric Railroaders Association, 1964).

From Canoe to Tunnel: a Sketch of the History of Transportation Between Jersey City and New York, 1661–1909 (Jersey City: The Free Library, 1909).

Garelick, Martin. "Rail Rebirth for New Jersey," *Progressive Railroading* 27 (August 1984), 29–34.

Hazelton, Hugh. "The New Steel Cars of the Hudson Companies," *Street Railway Journal* 30 (June 8, 1907), 1028–34.

———, "The Jersey City Yards and Shops of the Hudson & Manhattan Railroad," *Electric Railway Journal* 37 (May 6, 1911), 780–83.

"Hudson and Manhattan Railroad," *Electric Railroads*; 27 (August 1959).

McAdoo, William G. *Crowded Years: The Reminiscences of William G. McAdoo* (Port Washington, NY: Kennikat, 1931).

———, *The Relations Between Public Service Corporations and the Public* (New York: Alexander Hamilton Institute, 1910).

Middleton, William D. *Manhattan Gateway; New York's Pennsylvania Station*. (Waukesha, WI: Kalmbach, 1996).

———, *When the Steam Railroads Electrified* (Milwaukee: Kalmbach, 1974).

Nelligan, Tom, and Scott Hartley. *Trains of the Northeast Corridor* (New York: Quadrant, 1982).

"Opening of the Hudson River Tunnel System," *Street Railway Journal* 31 (February 29, 1908), 329–32.

"Opening of the Hudson River Tunnel System," *Scientific American* 97 (February 22, 1908), 124–26.

"Operating Practices of the Hudson Companies," *Electric Railway Journal* 37 (June 24, 1911), 1098–1104.

"PATH Puts It All Together," *Railway Age* 173 (July 10, 1972), 34–37.

Penn Central Railroad. "Multiple Unit Equipment in Penn Central Ownership" (rev. February 1, 1972). [Internal Penn Central working document.]

Pennsylvania Railroad. *Pennsylvania Station in New York City* (Philadelphia: The Pennsylvania Railroad, 1910).

———, "AC MU Cars—General Data," (rev. July 15, 1959). [Internal PRR working document.]

Pequinot, C. A. (ed.). *Tunnels and Tunneling* (London: Hutchinson, 1963).

Perelman, Carl. "Hudson-Bergen Light Rail Debut," *Railpace Newsmagazine* 19 (June 2000), 10–12.

Ramsey, William V. (ed.). *A Story of the Church Street Terminal Buildings of the Hudson & Manhattan Railroad Company* (New York: Wynkoop Hallenbeck Crawford, 1909).

Rohde, William L. "Sunnyside Yard," *Railroad* 45 (May 1948), 10–25.

Schafer, Mike, and Brian Solomon. *Pennsylvania Railroad* (Osceola, WI: MBI Publishing, 1997).

Seyfried, Vincent F. *The Long Island Rail Road*, vol. 6, The Age of Electrification, 1901–1916 (Garden City, NY: Vincent F. Seyfried, 1966).

Solomon, Brian. *Bullet Trains* (Osceola, WI: MBI Publishing, 2001).
Staufer, Alvin F., and Bert Pennypacker. *Pennsy Power* (Medina, OH: Staufer Litho Plate Company, 1962).
———, *Pennsy Power II* (Medina, OH: Staufer Litho Plate Company, 1968).
"Steel Cars for the Newark Extension of the Hudson Tunnels," *Street Railway Journal* 38 (August 12, 1911) 274–76.
"The Cortlandt Street Tunnels and Terminal Building, New York," *Scientific American* 96 (January 26, 1907), 88–89.
"The Passenger Stations of the Hudson Companies," *Street Railway Journal* 30 (March 9, 1907), 418–22.
"Traffic Promotion Work of the Hudson & Manhattan Railroad," *Street Railway Journal* 39 (November 25, 1911), 1090–94.
"Twenty Men Buried Alive," *The New York Times* (July 22, 1880).
Westing, Frederick. "GG1," *Trains* 24 (March 1964), 20–36.
———, "The Locomotive That Made Penn Station Possible," *Trains* 16 (October 1956), 28–38.
Zimmerman, Karl R. *The Remarkable GG1* (New York: Quadrant, 1977).

APPENDIX A

Rapid Transit Roster

HUDSON & MANHATTAN * PENNSYLVANIA R.R. * PATH

Numbers	Class	Year Built	Builder	Status	Notes
200–209	A	1908	Pressed Steel Car Company	retired	1
210–249	A	1908	American Car & Foundry (ACF)	retired	1
250–339	B	1909	Pressed Steel	retired	1, 10
340–389	C	1910	ACF	retired	1
701–736	D	1911	Pressed Steel	retired	1, 2
1901–1960	MP-38	1911	Pressed Steel	retired	3
401–425	E	1921	ACF	retired	1
426–450	F	1922	ACF	retired	1
451–457	G	1923	ACF	retired	1
801–804	H	1927	ACF	retired	1, 2
1961–1972	MP-38A	1927	ACF	retired	3
501–520	J	1928	ACF	retired	1, 11
1200–1229	MP-52	1958	St. Louis Car Company	retired	4, 6
1230–1249	K	1958	St. Louis	retired	5, 6
100–151	PA-1	1965	GSI-St. Louis	in service	6, 7, 8
600–706	PA-1	1965	GSI-St. Louis	in service	6, 7
152–181	PA-2	1967	GSI-St. Louis	in service	6, 7, 8
710–723	PA-2	1967	GSI-St. Louis	in service	6, 7
724–769	PA-3	1972	Hawker-Siddley	in service	6, 7
800–894	PA-4	1986	Kawasaki Heavy Industries	in service	6, 7, 9

NOTES

(1) Owned by Hudson & Manhattan R.R. and popularly known as "black cars."
(2) Owned by H&M; built to similar specifications as MP-38's and used in "joint service" to Newark; popularly known as "red cars," or "McAdoo reds."
(3) Owned by Pennsylvania R.R. and used in "joint service" to Newark; popularly known as "red cars," or "McAdoo reds."
(4) Originally owned by Pennsylvania R.R., later Penn Central; leased to PATH after "joint service" between Journal Square and Newark became a PATH-only responsibility (see text).
(5) Originally owned by Hudson & Manhattan R.R., later conveyed to PATH.
(6) Fully air-conditioned.
(7) Owned by PATH.
(8) Cab-less "C" cars; all other PA-class cars ("A" cars) feature operator's cab on one end only.
(9) Unfinished brushed aluminum car bodies and three sets of doors per side; all other PA-class cars have painted aluminum bodies with stainless steel trim and two sets of doors per side.
(10) Car No. 256 preserved at National Museum of Transport in St. Louis.
(11) Car No. 503 preserved at Shore Line Trolley Museum; car No. 510 and No. 513 preserved at Trolley Museum of New York.

Note: Many H&M "black cars" classes B, C, E, F, G and J were owned and operated by PATH between 1962 and arrival of PA-1 and PA-2 units.

APPENDIX B

Electric Locomotives

PENNSYLVANIA R.R. * NEW JERSEY TRANSIT * AMTRAK

Designation	Owner(s)	No. of Units	Builder (Date)	Notes
DD-1	PRR; LIRR	33	Juniata (1910–'11)	1, 2, 3
L-5	PRR	23	Juniata (1924–'28)	1, 2
O-1	PRR	8	Juniata (1930–'31)	4, 2
P-5	PRR	92	Juniata, Westinghouse & General Electric (1931–'35)	4, 2, 5
GG-1	PRR; Penn Central; Amtrak; NJT	139	Juniata & General Electric (1934–'43)	4, 2, 6
E60CP	Amtrak; NJT	26	General Electric (1975–'76)	4, 6, 8
AEM-7	Amtrak	53	Electro-Motive Division (1979–'88)	4, 7
ALP-44	NJT	20	ABB (1990–'95)	4, 7
ALP-44M	NJT	12	Adtranz (1996–'97)	4, 7
HHP-8	Amtrak	15	Alstom-Bombardier (2000–'01)	4, 7
Acela Power Cars	Amtrak	40	Alstom-Bombardier (2000–'01)	4, 7, 9
ALP-46	NJT	24	Adtranz (2001–'02)	4, 7, 10

NOTES

(1) Direct current electric locomotives operating from third rail.
(2) All units retired.
(3) Several DD-1 units ran on the Long Island R.R. after the PRR's ac electrification rendered them unnecessary on parent road. A single DD-1 has been preserved at the Railroad Museum of Pennsylvania in Strasburg, PA.
(4) Alternating current electric locomotives operating from overhead catenary.
(5) While initially used in passenger service, P-5 class locomotives spent majority of service life in freight service.
(6) Amtrak acquired 30 GG-1's and used additional Penn Central-owned units under lease. Amtrak-owned locomotives re-numbered in the 900-series from PRR's original 4800–4900 sequence. NJ Transit acquired 13 GG-1's, Nos. 4884 through 4872. A number of GG-1's that had been converted to freight locomotives were conveyed to Conrail by Penn Central. Several GG-1's have been preserved at various railroad museums.
(7) In service in 2001.
(8) Amtrak sold 10 locomotives to New Jersey Transit in 1984; all have since been retired. Amtrak-owned units expected to be retired ca. 2001 with the arrival of all HHP-8 units.

(9) Single-cab electric locomotives more commonly called power cars (see text); designed for use with new high-speed Acela trainsets.

(10) While NJT's ALP-44 and ALP-44M units are derived from Amtrak's AEM-7, ALP-46 units will be based on a contemporary German design.

Note: Amtrak and LIRR diesel-electric locomotives designed to draw dc current from third rail and that currently operate into and out of Penn Station are not included in this roster, nor are Amtrak trainsets that are primarily powered by gas turbine engines, but are also equipped with auxiliary electric motors for operation from Penn Station's dc third rail.

APPENDIX C

Railroad Electric Multiple-Unit Cars

PENNSYLVANIA R.R. * NEW JERSEY TRANSIT * AMTRAK

Designation	Owner(s)	No. of Units	Builder	Notes
MP-54	PRR	6	American Car & Foundry (1912)	1, 4
MP-54; MA 9 (see note 2)	PRR; Penn Central	434	PRR Altoona (354 cars; 1915–'34); Standard Steel Car Co. (49 cars; 1927); Pressed Steel Car Co. (15 cars; 1927); American Car & Foundry Co. (15 cars; 1927); PRR Wilmington (1 car; 1939)	2, 4
MP-54; MA9 (see note 2)	PRR; Penn Central	100	50 MP-54 cars re-built by PRR in Wilmington as class MP-54E5 (1950–'53); 49 P-54 coaches and 1 MP-54 un-powered trailer unit re-built by PRR in Altoona as class MP54E6 (1950–'51)	2, 3, 4
MP-85	(see note 5)	4	Budd (1958)	5
MP-85; MA1-A "Jersey Arrow" "Arrow I"	NJ DOT; NJ Transit	35	St. Louis Car Co. (1968)	6
MR1-A; MS1-A "Metrolines"	Penn Central; Amtrak	61	Budd (1968)	7
MA1-G "Arrow II"	NJ DOT; NJ Transit	70	AVCO/General Electric (1974–'75)	4
MA1-H "Arrow-III"	NJ Transit	30	AVCO/General Electric (1977–'78)	8
MA1-J "Arrow-III"	NJ Transit	200	AVCO/General Electric (1978)	8

NOTES

(1) Four coaches and two combination coach-baggage cars used in third rail d.c. service between Penn Station and Manhattan Transfer; conveyed to LIRR in 1923, later retired.

(2) MP-54 was the common designation for PRR 64-foot electric multiple-unit cars, although there were sub-classes with separate designations. Seven all-baggage models were designated MB-62 units, 8 baggage-mail cars were MBM-62 units, while 57 combination coach-baggage cars were identified MPB-54. Toward the end of their service life in the 1970's, remaining MP-54 cars were re-designated MA9 units. The MP-54 fleet did not operate exclusively out of Penn Station; it also provided suburban service in the Philadelphia area, as well as between Baltimore and Washington. Of the 434 cars built before the Second World War, 43 MP-54 passenger cars and 4 MBM-62 baggage-mail cars were un-powered trailer units.

(3) Because this re-build project during the early 1950's involved 51 older MP-54

electric multiple-unit cars and 49 P-54 suburban passenger coaches that were never previously part of the MP-54 fleet, there has been confusion over the total number of MP-54 electric cars owned by PRR. A review of PRR documents suggests the railroad owned 483 separate and different alternating current MP-54 cars over the years, a number that includes MB-62's, MPB-54's, and other such sub-classes.

(4) All retired.
(5) Owned by U.S. Office of High-Speed Ground Transportation and used for testing. Not known to have been used in revenue passenger service; included in roster for interest's sake. Numbered T-1, T-2, T-3 AND T-4.
(6) Built as electric multiple-unit cars; MP-85 designation changed to MA1 circa 1970. *Arrow I* fleet later converted into locomotive-hauled cars.
(7) Equipment used to inaugurate high-speed Metroliner service between New York and Washington in 1969. Built and delivered with PRR markings, but did not enter revenue service until after Penn Central merger. Some units later used in e.m.u. service between Philadelphia and Harrisburg. Nos. 800–830 designated class MR1-A, while Nos. 850–869 were class MS1-A. Many currently out of service while as many as 30 remained in service circa 2001 as un-powered control cab units to allow locomotive-hauled trains to operate in bi-directional fashion. Originally, 50 cars were intended for Northeast Corridor service between Washington and New York and eleven for service between Philadelphia and Harrisburg under the auspices of the state of Pennsylvania. Pennsylvania support failed to materialize and all 61 cars were assigned to Washington-New York service. Car No. 820 preserved at the Railroad Museum of Pennsylvania, in Strasburg.
(8) Only e.m.u. cars in service into and out of New York's Penn Station circa 2001; rebuilt with new propulsion systems in early 1990's.

Note: Direct current third-rail e.m.u. cars operated in Penn Station service by the Long Island R.R. not included in this roster. Likewise excluded are publicly-owned e.m.u. cars that provide suburban service in the Philadelphia area but occasionally operate into and out of Penn Station, as well as e.m.u. cars from the former New York, New Haven and Hartford R.R. that saw some Penn Station service as locomotive-hauled cars following Penn Central merger.

APPENDIX D

*Departures from Penn Station
via the Hudson River Tunnels
Weekdays—Summer 2001
5:00 PM through 6:00 PM*

Time	Train	Operator	Destination	Service
5:00	123	AMTK	Washington	Metroliner
5:03	3863	NJT	Trenton	Northeast Corridor
5:06	3725	NJT	Jersey Avenue	Northeast Corridor
5:09	189	AMTK	Washington	Northeast Direct
5:12	3607	NJT	South Amboy	North Jersey Coast
5:15	627	AMTK	Philadelphia	Clocker
5:18	6647	NJT	Dover	Midtown Direct
5:20	6431	NJT	Gladstone	Midtown Direct
5:24	3865	NJT	Trenton	Northeast Corridor
5:27	3267	NJT	Long Branch	North Jersey Coast
5:30	3609	NJT	South Amboy	North Jersey Coast
5:33	3269	NJT	Long Branch	North Jersey Coast
5:36	3727	NJT	Jersey Avenue	Northeast Corridor
5:39	173	AMTK	Washington	Northeast Direct
5:42	629	AMTK	Philadelphia	Clocker
5:45	6435	NJT	Gladstone	Midtown Direct
5:48	6651	NJT	Dover	Midtown Direct
5:52	3729	NJT	Jersey Avenue	Northeast Corridor
5:55	3271	NJT	Long Branch	North Jersey Coast
6:00	125	AMTK	Washington	Metroliner

NOTES

(1) Nominal one-way capacity of Hudson River tunnels circa 2001 was said to be 18 trains per hour. Summer 2001 time tables actually called for 19, however, with most departures scheduled three minutes after the preceding train. Metroliners, as well as Acela Express schedules, were typically accorded a five-minute window between their departure and that of the preceding train. All data derived from Amtrak (AMTK) and New Jersey Transit (NJT) summer 2001 public timetables

(2) In addition to trains shown, AMTK No. 265 departed Penn Station for Albany-Rensselaer at 5:50 PM. While this train operated via the West Side Connection and did not use Hudson River tunnels, its departure often impacted smooth operation of NJT schedules.

www.ingramcontent.com/pod-product-compliance
Lightning Source LLC
Chambersburg PA
CBHW051455290426
44109CB00016B/1766